AGGRESSIVE

AND

VIOLENT

STUDENTS

Written by: Robert Bowman, Jo Lynn Johnson,
Michael Paget, & Mary Thomas-Williams

Cover Design & Project Layout by Elizabeth Madden
Project Editing by Susan Bowman & Melissa White

ISBN 1-889636-16-9

Library of Congress Number 99-60009

10 9 8 7 6 5 4 3 2
Printed in the United States of America

TABLE OF CONTENTS

Section I:

Overview

"*Knowledge is the anecdote to fear . . .*"
Ralph Waldo Emerson

2

Philosophy

We believe that schools can and should be peaceful places where children can learn and grow, nurtured by staff that understands and practices the skills of peace keeping.

We believe that children can be taught to manage both feelings and behaviors in ways that are nonviolent and pro-social, and that these skills will lead to healthy productive citizens.

We believe that through practice of primary prevention and early intervention strategies, staff can foster an environment that is conducive to learning and models the behavior expected of young people.

We further believe that we must all work toward making a peaceful world by employing peace keeping skills at all levels of society and in our daily lives.

Introduction

No school, whether small or large, rural or suburban, elementary, middle, or high is immune to violence. Crime and violence pervade schools across our nation.

Knowing that violence in schools is merely a reflection of violence in society is of little comfort to teachers and administrators. Acts of violence disrupt the normal functioning of a school and prevents students and teachers from concentrating on meaningful learning and teaching. Therefore, *Aggressive and Violent Students* focuses on skills and strategies that promote pro-social behavior and help deter crime and misbehavior in schools. *Aggressive and Violent Students* is divided into sections:

Section I: Overview

Section II: The Do's and Don'ts of Building a Safe School

Section III: Five Powerful Strategies for Managing and Surviving Hostile or Aggressive Students

Section IV: Teaching Students the Steps to Anger Management and Control, Conflict Resolution, Creative Assertiveness, "Bully Fighting," and Peer Mediation

Section V: Managing and Surviving Classroom Crises

Ground Rules or Norms

Social systems (countries, students, agencies and families) have agreed upon rules by which they operate. They are called laws, policies, rules, norms or boundaries. These rules define limits, establish normative behavior and, provide security and safety. Without them there would be chaos. Providing clear limits for students whether school-wide in the classroom or in a school counseling group is critical.

Setting limits that are fair, equitable and enforced are important as protective factors for the growth and well-being of young people. Research has identified a lack of limits as a risk predictor for adolescent problem behavior. Systems (whether family or school) put a child at risk if the discipline or behavior management is chaotic (no limits) or conversely harsh, punitive and rigid. Therefore establishing clear risks for behavior, enforcing them fairly and, invoking consequences for violations provide a model for pro-social behavior and create an environment of safety and trust.

Students are more likely to agree to and be invested in rules or norms in which they have had some impact. Honoring their wisdom by allowing them to participate in the development of a code of conduct or classroom norms gives them a sense of ownership and experience in negotiating what they and their school may value regarding appropriate behavior.

Counselors, teachers and administrators who allow students to take part in the development of rules are not giving away their power but rather <u>sharing</u> their power. It is important for adults to be candid about what <u>must</u> be and what is negotiable.

Some things to consider for developing and using ground rules:

1. State clearly what parts of the code of conduct, etc. are open for discussion and which parts are not.
2. Be clear about consequences regarding violations.
3. Work at the list of norms until <u>all</u> can agree. The time it may take is worth it.
4. When consensus is reached, consider having the class or group sign them.
5. Review them often.
6. Create a process for discussing them with a new group or class members.
7. Post them.
8. Assess your attention to them
9. Confront behaviors which violate them.
10. Revise them as needed you may not need them all!
11. Use them to build a community.
12. Trust the wisdom of the group to create and use the rules well!

Statistics on Violence

- More than 100,000 students carry guns to school every day (Wilson-Brewer *et al.*, 1991).

- In one survey, 85 percent of Canadian students considered youth violence a serious problem (*People Against Youth Violence*, 1993).

- The Los Angeles County school district reported more than 2,200 hate crimes in a single year (O'Neill, 1993).

- In one study, 60 percent of the boys who were characterized as bullies in grade 6 through grade 9 had a least one conviction by the age of 24 (Olweus, 1992).

- Every 19 seconds a teen in the United States is a victim of crime (Zimmer, 1988).

- In a study of teenagers, 83 percent reported they had witnessed students in fist fights (*USA Today*, May 20, 1992).

- Approximately 2 million children in the United States are seriously abused annually.

- At least 1,000 children die annually as a result of their injuries.

- Approximately every five (5) seconds, someone is a victim of assault and battery, gunshot wounds, rape, gang attacks, robbery, incest and automobile crashes due to Driving Under the Influence (DUI).

- It is estimated that $5 billion to $10 billion a year is spent on treating victims of family violence.

- Most victims are attacked or victimized by a member of their own family.

- One out of 4 (1 in 4) households will be affected by violence this year.

- Destructive school behaviors such as vandalism, violence and truancy correlated with student use of alcohol and other drug use. Users are:
  - ☞ More than twice as likely to get into physical fights; 50% of users admitted initiating violence.

  - ☞ Four (4) times more likely to commit vandalism; 54% of users say they destroy things for fun.

  - ☞ Twice as likely to have trouble concentrating in class.

  - ☞ Three times more likely to be truant from school

In 1991 the Department of Justice issued the results of a six-month study conducted in 1988-1989 showing that 2 percent of students twelve to nineteen were victims of violent offenses. The study found that public school students were more likely to be victims than students in private schools, and ninth-grade students were victimized more than students in all higher grades.

Sixteen percent reported incidents of a student attacking or threatening a teacher. Thirty-one percent said that alcohol was easy to obtain at or near school; 47 percent said it was hard or impossible to obtain. In reference to drugs, 30 percent said it was easy to obtain marijuana; 11 percent, cocaine; and 9 percent, crack. Forty-three percent said it was hard or impossible to obtain marijuana; 58 percent, cocaine; and 57 percent, crack. Close to two percent of the students admitted that they had carried weapons to school to protect themselves. Those weapons included guns, knives, brass knuckles, razor blades, and spiked jewelry.

- Violence has replaced infection as the leading killer of young people in the United States.

- Some 23,000 people are murdered in the United States each year -- roughly 400 a week, or one every half hour. Most of the victims know their assailant.

About a third of the victims are killed by total strangers, sometimes for no apparent reason.

- People younger than eighteen commit a quarter of the violent crime, and they are more likely than adults to do so in gangs of three or more.

- The number of murders committed by young people between the ages of fifteen and twenty-four has more than doubled over the past twenty-five years. Most violent crimes are, in fact, committed by this age group.

- More than 80,000 forcible rapes occur in a year.

- Nearly 25 million households experience a crime of violence or theft in any given year.

- More than 100,000 teachers are physically assaulted by students every year.

- According to the Federal Bureau of Investigation, about 46 percent of all violent crimes reported during 1987 were committed by youths between the ages of ten and twenty-four.

More Statistics

From APA, *Violence and Youth: Psychology's Response*, 1993.

- Homicide is the most common cause of death for young African American females and males.

- Guns are involved in more than 75% of adolescent killings.

- In a study of first and second graders in Washington, D.C., 45% had witnessed muggings, 31% had witnessed shootings, and 39% said they had seen dead bodies.

- The United States has the highest homicide rate of any Western industrialized society. It is estimated that 40% -50% of American households have guns; half of these are handguns.

- Students carry an estimated 270,000 handguns to school every day.

- Between 1979 and 1989 there was a 61% increase in homicides by shootings committed by youth.

- Alcohol is a factor in about 65% of all homicides.

- Alcohol is a factor in about 55% of all assaults in the home.

From *The Index of Leading Cultural Indicators*, by William Bennett, 1994.

- In 1940 teachers identified the major problems in school to be talking out of turn, chewing gum, making noise, running in the halls, cutting in line, dress code infractions, and littering; in 1990 they identified drug abuse, alcohol abuse, pregnancy, suicide, rape, robbery, and assault.

- From 1965 to 1990 the arrest rate for violent juvenile crime tripled.

- Between 1982 and 1991 the arrest rate for juveniles for murder increased 93%; for aggravated assault 72%; for forcible rape 24%; and for motor vehicle theft 97%.

- 70% of the teenagers in long-term correctional facilities grew up in a household without a father.

- In 1960, 9.1% of families were single parent; in 1991, 28.6% of families were single parent.

- Children from single-parent families are 2 to 3 times as likely to develop emotional and behavioral problems as do children in two-parent families.

- Since 1960 the rate of suicide among youth has tripled.

- The average child watches up to 8,000 made for TV murders and 100,000 acts of violence by the end of grade school.

From The South Carolina Education Association newsletter, "The SCEA Emphasis," August, 1994.

- Nearly 50,000 children were killed by firearms between 1979 and 1991, equal to the number of American casualties in the Vietnam War. • Every two hours a child dies from gunshot wounds; every day 30 children are injured by gun violence.

- Each day 1.2 million latchkey children come home to an unsupervised house in which there is a gun.

From the *Journal of Safe Management of Disruptive and Assaultive Behavior*, April, 1994.

- During the 1980's there were 16 incidents of mass murder in the workplace; in the first three years of the 1990's there have been 21 such incidents.

What Students Think

65,000 STUDENTS RESPOND

The results of this survey are based on the written answers of 65,193 sixth through twelfth graders who responded individually or as classes to a questionnaire by the National Association of Secondary School Principals in the August 13-15, 1993 USA WEEKEND.

OVERALL

- 37% of students don't feel safe in school.
- 50% know someone who switched schools to feel safer.

VIOLENCE AND THEFT

- 43% of public school kids avoid school restrooms.
- 26% of girls, 49% of boys were hit last year at school.
- 76% say lockers aren't a safe place for valuables.
- 27% of girls were sexually harassed last year.

WORRIES AND LEARNING

- 63% say they'd learn more if they felt safer.
- 47% say teachers spend at least half of the class time disciplining students.
- 41% of students think about their safety at least a quarter of the day.

CAUSES AND SOLUTIONS

- 55% in grade 10-12 know weapons are regularly in school.
- 79% say violence often is caused by "stupid" things like bumping into someone.
- 49% in grades 10-12 say race often is a factor in violence.
- 37% say students who hurt others should be required to do community service.
- 23% want antiviolence classes.
- 13% want metal detectors.

Violence & the Media

Violence On TV

Comparing violence on a number of broadcast outlets, a study by the Center for Media and Public Affairs analyzes the programming (including commercials) during a "typical day" of American television in one major market -- Washington, D.C. -- from 6:00 am. to midnight on April 2, 1992. A total of 1,846 individual violent acts were recorded, including 175 scenes involving one or more deaths on the 10 channels analyzed: affiliates of ABC, CBS, NBC, FOX, and PBS; independent commercial station WDCA; and cable channels WTBS, the USA Network, MTV, and HBO. PBS registered the fewest incidents of violence. The rankings are as follows:

WTBS	321 scenes	(18 per hour)
HBO	257 scenes	(14 per hour)
USA	209 scenes	(12 per hour)
MTV	202 scenes	(11 per hour)
FOX	182 scenes	(10 per hour)
CBS	175 scenes	(10 per hour)
ABC	48 scenes	(3 per hour)
NBC	39 scenes	(3 per hour)
PBS	37 scenes	(2 per hour)

In a single day, television programs depict 1,800 individual acts of violence (Hickey, 1992). A recent study of 1,100 children found that the more time a child spent viewing television, the more he or she displayed troubled or violent behavior, such as disobedience, bullying, and aggression (Venbrux, 1993; *USA Today*, May 24, 1993).

Research has shown that teenagers are influenced not only by the violence on television and the media's glorification of bullying behavior, but also by the violent acts they witness in their own homes and communities. Some teens imitate this behavior (Goldstein, 1991).

Years of research evidence has gone into establishing television violence as a contributing cause to violence in our society -- and the word 'cause' is not used lightly by scientists."

Ronald Slaby
Senior Scientist
The Education Development Center

"Dr. Leonard Eron, University of Illinois said in testimony before Congress, "that there is no longer any doubt that heavy exposure to televised violence is one of the causes of aggressive behavior, crime, and violence in society, and he estimates that fully 10% of the actual violence in our society is attributable to the viewing of violence on television."

The Chemical People
Spring 1993

"We have to make a distinction between violence that is selectively used, violence that is handcrafted to show its tragic consequences, to show the pain and to show the suffering and the tragedy that follows. We're talking about mass-produced cheap, industrial violence that's injected into every home whether they like it or not."

George Gerbner
Dean Emeritus, Annenberg School of Communications
University of Pennsylvania

"When characters like Rambo get angry, they blow people away. So children have learned that violence is the way to solve problems."

Deborah Prothrow-Stith, M.D.
Harvard School of Public Health

"In the media world, brutality is portrayed as ordinary and amusing."

Deadly Consequences
Deborah Prothrow-Stith, M.D.

SUPER BOWL SUNDAY -- Hundreds of thousands of battered and abused women call the National Domestic Violence Hotline, making Super Bowl Sunday the hotline's busiest day of the year.

American Medical Association Auxiliary, Inc.

Not the Cause

Domestic violence counselors hear it all the time: "He only beats me when he's drunk" or "I only do this when I'm drunk." Is it the alcohol -- or is alcohol just an excuse?"

Alcohol is a cofactor in domestic violence, not a cause. It aggravates situations.

It's not just the alcohol use of the abuser in domestic violence situations. Studies of battered women have found between 7 and 14 percent to be alcoholic. Alcohol use by the victim also leads to excuses.

Prevention File
Special Edition 1992

"An abused person will reach out to someone just to talk, but won't directly accuse the abuser, who is usually a loved one."

American Medical Association Auxiliary, Inc.

"Up to 35% of women who visit the emergency room are there because of violence-related injuries."

American Medical Association, Auxiliary FACETS
March 1992

"One in four girls and one in six boys are sexually abused before the age of 18."

The Brown University Child and Adolescent Behavior Letter
Vol. 8, No. 11
November 1992

"Half of all homicide victims are killed by people they know."

Antonia Novello, MD, MPH

"Risk behaviors taken by adolescents in reaction to abuse, such as running away, increased sexual activity, or substance use multiply the dangers to their health."

Target 2000
Vol/3, No. 1, Summer 1992

"Youth gangs (comprised of core leaders, regulars, peripheral members, and 'wannabees') serve as a basis for recruitment and even a potential infrastructure for adult criminal enterprises."

Special Report
Gangs and Our Youth
University of Pittsburgh
Office of Child Development

"A tie that binds gang members is the broken homes they come from and their lack of place in the community."

Milwaukee Journal

"If we don't deal with the adolescents as victims, we will ultimately have to deal with large numbers of them as perpetrators."

James Garbarino

"Hospital costs related to firearm injuries added an estimated $429 million to health care costs each year. When ambulance services, physician fees, rehabilitation, and long-term care costs are included, total medical expenditures for firearm injuries reaches an estimated $1 billion per year."

AMA, Auxiliary FACETS
March 1992

"One-fourth of all American families are touched by violence each year."

AMA Auxiliary, Inc.

"Nearly 7 out of 10 manslaughter offenses occur after a person has been drinking or using other drugs."

CSAP

Family Violence

Termed the disease of the '90s, violence is as complex and life threatening as any of the killer diseases of the past two centuries. It touches as many as one-fourth of all American households. But, as serious as the overall problem is, of greater concern is that violence often occurs between family members -- parents and children, husbands and wives, brothers and sisters.

Who are the victimizers?

Potential abusers come from all economic, racial, ethnic, and religious groups. They can be male or female, adolescents, or adults. Consider these facts.

• Three siblings in 100 use weapons on sisters or brothers, meaning that 100,000 children in the United States annually face brothers and sisters with guns or knives in hand.

• Six out of 10 couples have experienced violence at some time during their marriages, with either husbands beating wives or vice versa.

• Approximately 900,000 parents are beaten or abused by their children each year.

• Child homicide is now among the five leading causes of death in childhood, with the majority of infant victims killed by parents, relatives, and older children.

Woman & Violence

• Esta Soler, executive director of the Family Violence Prevention Fund, believes the role of alcohol in domestic violence contributes to society's perception that it is not a serious problem. "Domestic violence is hidden behind other social problems, most notably alcohol and other drug use."

• Alcohol advertisers use female body parts or (send) violent messages such as "if your date won't listen to reason, try a Velvet Hammer.

- Karen Hughes, associate director for alcohol policy at the Trauma Foundation in San Francisco, shares Soler's opinion of alcohol advertising. She described a new project -- called *We've Had Enough* -- in San Francisco and Los Angeles designed to break the link between sex and violence and alcohol.

- "The goal of this project is to eliminate slogans and images in alcohol advertising that condone or trivialize violence against women." Any reduction in domestic violence will require changes in social norms that reinforce violence, particularly violence against women.

Prevention File
Special Edition 1992

Teen Violence

- Every day 14 children aged 19 and under are killed with firearms. In 1995, over 5,200 children aged 1-19 were killed by guns. Firearm injuries are the second leading cause of death for youth aged 10-24 nationwide.

- The Department of Justice reported that the number of non-firearm juvenile homicide victims increased by 9% between 1985 and 1995, while the number of juveniles murdered with firearms increased by 153%. Guns make it easy to kill, far easier than with any other weapon commonly available.

- In 1995, 83% of homicides for juvenile victims aged 12 and over involved firearms.

Ceasefire Action Network Newsletter
Vol. 14, July 1998

	BEST	WORST
Juvenile Violent Crime Arrest Rate	Vermont	District of Columbia
Percent Graduating from High School	Connecticut	Arizona & Nebraska
Percent of Teens Not in School and Not in the Labor Force	North Dakota	West Virginia
Teen Violent Death Rate	Maine	District of Columbia
Percent of Children in Poverty	New Hampshire & Utah	District of Columbia

Kids Count Data Book, 1995
The Annie E. Casey Foundation
Baltimore, MD

Victimization

- Eight out of 10 Americans can expect to be victims of violent crimes at least once in their lives.

- 99% of Americans will be victims of theft at least once in their lives.

- Teenagers are 2.5 times more likely to be victims of violent crimes than those over age 20.

- About 3 million thefts and violent crimes occur on or near a school campus each year, representing 16,000 incidents per day.

- A study of 8th graders in Chicago revealed that 73% had seen someone shot, stabbed, robbed, or killed.

Personal Observation

Like a stone thrown in a pond, victimization goes beyond the actual incident of personal physical harm; if you are the victim of violence the physical and psychological effects are obvious; if you know someone who is the victim of violence, the effects to yourself are more subtle, but no less real. You may become more cautious in your relationships, in where you go, in how you spend your time. And even if you simply hear of someone who is a victim, it undermines your sense of security.

Meeting Our Basic Needs

Attempting to eliminate aggressive and violent behavior in youth without first looking at the basic needs of youth is like building a house without a foundation. We begin with the assumption that all people have basic needs that need to be addressed. Further, when those needs are not addressed it increases the likelihood of inappropriate behavior. Major personality theorists have proposed models of human basic needs. Following is a summary of the work of one of those theorists, Dr. William Glasser.

Purpose

1. To allow students to identify how they meet their basic needs

2. To assess the positive and negative ways needs are being met

3. To recognize the climate needed to meet basic needs

Procedures

1. Give students an explanation and example of the 4 psychological needs.

2. Ask students to fill out My Basic Needs Sheet.

3. Answer questions on basic needs handout.

Follow-Up

1. Pair students and ask them to share 2 items from their sheets.

2. Ask each pair to identify an example of the basic needs that could happen in the classroom -- students' and teachers' basic needs.

3. Design, develop or create a classroom that meets the basic needs of teachers and students. (What does the classroom look like, sound like, feel like?)

Basic Needs
(Student)

Place a check mark on the continuum that denotes whether your needs are met or not.

		Needs Not Met			Needs Met Completely	
		1	2	3	4	5
BELONGING						
	a. home	❑	❑	❑	❑	❑
	b. school	❑	❑	❑	❑	❑
	c. friends	❑	❑	❑	❑	❑
POWER						
	a. home	❑	❑	❑	❑	❑
	b. school	❑	❑	❑	❑	❑
	c. friends	❑	❑	❑	❑	❑
FREEDOM						
	a. home	❑	❑	❑	❑	❑
	b. school	❑	❑	❑	❑	❑
	c. friends	❑	❑	❑	❑	❑
FUN						
	a. home	❑	❑	❑	❑	❑
	b. school	❑	❑	❑	❑	❑
	c. friends	❑	❑	❑	❑	❑

1. In what areas are your needs being satisfactorily met?

2. In the areas that you are not satisfied or pleased, what would help?

3. What are some concrete steps you can take to meet your needs?

4. Examine your continuum above and see how many of the needs are above 3 and how many are below. What are the implications for you in this activity?

Adapted from: Glasser, William (1986) Control Theory in the Classroom. NY: Harper and Row

Basic Needs
(Staff)

Place a check mark on the continuum that denotes whether your needs are met or not.

	Needs Not Met			Needs Met Completely	
	1	2	3	4	5
BELONGING					
Student	❑	❑	❑	❑	❑
Staff	❑	❑	❑	❑	❑
POWER					
Student	❑	❑	❑	❑	❑
Staff	❑	❑	❑	❑	❑
FREEDOM					
Student	❑	❑	❑	❑	❑
Staff	❑	❑	❑	❑	❑
FUN					
Student	❑	❑	❑	❑	❑
Staff	❑	❑	❑	❑	❑

1. What are the strengths at your school for meeting basic needs of students and staff?

2. In what ways do we need to change or grow in order to better meet the needs of our students?

3. What are some concrete steps you can take to help students meet their needs in your classroom?

4. Choose a partner and share one change that you will make (personally or professionally) to meet basic needs.

Adapted from: Glasser, William (1986) Control Theory in the Classroom. NY: Harper and Row

"It is better to teach a child, than to try to rehabilitate an adult"

Jo Lynn Johnson

"The only thing more expensive than education is ignorance.."

Anonymous

"Unlearning is harder than learning"

Anonymous

Section II:

The Do's and Don'ts of Building a Safe School

School-Wide Risk Inventory for Violence

Directions: **Read each statement and mark the appropriate response in the corresponding space.**

A. BUILDING

		Yes	No
1.	Is there adequate interior lighting for classrooms, hallways, bathrooms and locker rooms?	❏	❏
2.	Is maintenance consistent and timely for replacement and/or repairs of broken windows, damaged/broken locks, light fixtures?	❏	❏
3.	Is the school size adequate to support student population?	❏	❏
4.	Is school size small enough to build a sense of belonging and a sense of community?	❏	❏
5.	Does the school adequately monitor high risk time and places, such as:		
	a. class transition	❏	❏
	b. before/after school	❏	❏
	c. bathrooms	❏	❏
	d. cafeteria	❏	❏
	e. sport events and other functions	❏	❏
	f. assemblies	❏	❏
	g. playgrounds	❏	❏
6.	Is the school prepared to respond to a rapid increase or decrease in student enrollment?	❏	❏
7.	Are temporary classrooms accessible to:		
	a. building administrators' help	❏	❏
	b. telephone	❏	❏
	c. alarms	❏	❏
8.	Are temporary classrooms adequately equipped with:		
	a. telephones	❏	❏
	b. alarms	❏	❏
9.	Are temporary classrooms located close to the main building?	❏	❏
10.	Is building free of graffiti and litter?	❏	❏
11.	Is building adequately monitored?		
	a. metal detectors	❏	❏
	b. cameras	❏	❏
	c. alarm system	❏	❏
	d. telephones	❏	❏
	e. walkie-talkies	❏	❏

A. BUILDING Continued

		Yes	No
12.	Is the school located in a low crime area?	❏	❏
13.	Is there adequate outside lighting?	❏	❏
14.	Is landscape design conducive to a safe environment (i.e., good visibility)?	❏	❏
15.	Is landscaping of shrubs maintained for safety purposes?	❏	❏
16.	Are grounds free of graffiti and litter?	❏	❏

B. PERSONNEL

		Yes	No
1.	Is personnel adequate to handle increase in student enrollment?	❏	❏
2.	Are new students assigned to a staff as an advisor, contact or mentor?	❏	❏
3.	Is there adequate security/staff or personnel to monitor isolated (outside) areas?	❏	❏
4.	Is personnel adequate to monitor high risk time and locations, such as:		
	a. cafeteria	❏	❏
	b. hallways	❏	❏
	c. sport events	❏	❏
	d. playgrounds	❏	❏
	e. bathrooms	❏	❏
	f. class transitions	❏	❏

C. ADMINISTRATION

		Yes	No
1.	Does administration promote two-way communication?	❏	❏
2.	Does administration treat staff fairly and equitably?	❏	❏
3.	Does the administration model effective conflict resolution skills?	❏	❏
4.	Does administration involve parents and community in every aspect of the school?	❏	❏
5.	Does the administration support and value professional development and growth opportunities for staff in violence prevention and intervention programming?	❏	❏
6.	Is administration an integral part of violence prevention/intervention staff development?	❏	❏
7.	Is there supervision and support to ensure implementation and maintenance of violence prevention and intervention programming?	❏	❏
8.	Does the administration provide funding for violence prevention and intervention programs?	❏	❏

D. PROGRAMMING

		Yes	No
1.	Is there a K-12 age appropriate (scope and sequence) violence prevention curriculum?	❏	❏
2.	Is violence prevention/early intervention integrated into the core curricula?	❏	❏
3.	Is there a variety of educational options and alternatives that address the needs of all students?	❏	❏
4.	Are the curriculum approaches research and theory based?	❏	❏
5.	Does the program include conflict resolution for staff, students and parents?	❏	❏
6.	Are special assemblies and media campaigns used to address expected norms of behaviors prior to high risk events?	❏	❏
7.	Does a comprehensive violence prevention program for students which emphasizes knowledge, attitude and behavioral changes exist?	❏	❏
8.	Does the program address the unique needs of high risk students?	❏	❏
9.	Is the program sensitive to gender, ethnicity and cultural issues?	❏	❏
10.	Does the program include skill building and problem-solving anger management communication skills and assertiveness?	❏	❏
11.	Does the program address the legal consequences associated with violence?	❏	❏
12.	Does the orientation for new students and their parents contain information about violence prevention/intervention strategies, efforts and policy?	❏	❏
13.	Are student organizations encouraged to do programs related to violence prevention/intervention?	❏	❏
14.	Are students encouraged to become involved in activities that promote pro-social behaviors?	❏	❏
15.	Are service learning projects encouraged and supported by the administration and the school?	❏	❏
16.	Are violence prevention/intervention resources available in an accessible and non-threatening location?	❏	❏
17.	Does the program address violence prevention from a positive stance?	❏	❏
18.	Are there a variety of special programs designed to reduce risk factors and maximize protective factors for the prevention/intervention of violence, such as:		
	a. peer mediation	❏	❏
	b. conflict resolution	❏	❏
	c. school court	❏	❏
	d. mentoring	❏	❏

D. PROGRAMMING Continued

		Yes	No
e.	tutoring	❏	❏
f.	peer helping	❏	❏
g.	career preparation	❏	❏
h.	advisor-advisee (teacher advisement program TAP)	❏	❏

19. Is there a parent component to the violence prevention/intervention program? ❏ ❏

20. Is there support for creativity in development and delivery of curriculum? ❏ ❏

21. Is there adequate supervision and feedback for program delivery? ❏ ❏

E. POLICY/PROCEDURES

1. Does the policy address and support a safe learning environment for its students and staff? ❏ ❏

2. Does the policy reflect the standards and values of its community? ❏ ❏

3. Is there a rationale or philosophy that supports the policy? ❏ ❏

4. Does the policy recognize that prevention is the foundation for quality programming? ❏ ❏

5. Is the policy consistent with state/local law? ❏ ❏

6. Does the policy formulation or revision process involve the active participation of teacher, staff, parents, students and other relevant constituencies? ❏ ❏

7. Is the policy reviewed on an annual basis for updating or revision? ❏ ❏

8. Is the policy communicated to teachers, staff, students and parents on a regular basis? ❏ ❏

9. Is the policy administered fairly and equitably? ❏ ❏

10. Does the policy reflect a proactive approach to discipline? ❏ ❏

11. Does the policy allow for alternatives to suspension, detention, isolation and expulsion? ❏ ❏

12. Is there a crisis management plan in place? ❏ ❏

13. Is the role of all staff clearly defined in the utilization of the crisis management plan? ❏ ❏

14. Is the crisis management plan reviewed, revised or refined each year? ❏ ❏

15. Are referral procedures in place for all staff and students regarding anger management, conflict resolution and inappropriate behavior? ❏ ❏

E. POLICY/PROCEDURES Continued

		Yes	No
16.	Is there a communication network established in the event of violence impacting on the school?	❏	❏
17.	Is school policy that governs student assistant programs inclusive of potentially violent behavior?	❏	❏
18.	Does the school take adequate measures to restrict access to school grounds by unauthorized visitors?	❏	❏
19.	Is there a safe school plan in place?	❏	❏
20.	Are locker entry procedures for weapons and drugs clearly defined?	❏	❏
21.	Does the policy prohibit the display and wearing of clothing and paraphernalia that is representative of gangs or rival groups?	❏	❏
22.	Does the policy prohibit the display of clothing and paraphernalia that is exploitative or denigrating of gender, culture and race, (i.e., display of KKK, Confederate flags, tee shirts that reference females in an exploitative or abusive manner.)	❏	❏
23.	Does policy prevent students from leaving campus during lunch?	❏	❏
24.	Are procedures for search and seizure in place?	❏	❏
25.	Are students and their parents aware of these procedures and their right to privacy in writing?	❏	❏
26.	Are there procedures for communication with parents about their children's behavior on a regular basis?	❏	❏
27.	Does the school have a student assistant program?	❏	❏
28.	Does the school identify changes in student behavior such as, changes in performance, appearance, attitude, behavior and attendance?	❏	❏
29.	Are procedures in place for medical-related emergencies?	❏	❏
30.	Does the school policy support non-violence by abolishing corporal punishment?	❏	❏

F. STAFF DEVELOPMENT

		Yes	No
1.	Is there a comprehensive staff development plan for violence prevention/ intervention in place?	❏	❏
2.	Do all staff and administrators attend trainings to obtain up-to-date information on violence?	❏	❏

F. STAFF DEVELOPMENT Continued

	Yes	No
3. Do all staff receive training in the early identification of students who are at risk for violent behavior?	❏	❏
4. Do teachers, administrators and staff receive training on the limits of their authority with regard to confrontations, searches and confiscations?	❏	❏
5. Do teachers, administrators and staff receive training on when and how to deal with violence-related medical emergencies?	❏	❏
6. Do teachers, administrators and staff receive training on how and when to make appropriate referrals?	❏	❏

G. CLASS/SCHOOL CLIMATE

	Yes	No
1. Does the school climate enhance the academic self-image of students?	❏	❏
2. Do students feel safer and welcome in the school?	❏	❏
3. Are the school and class rules clearly stated?	❏	❏
4. Are school and class rules consistently enforced?	❏	❏
5. Are there clearly stated consequences for violation of rules?	❏	❏
6. Do teachers and staff model positive behaviors and use of skills?	❏	❏
7. Is there parental support for standards of discipline and modeling of positive behaviors?	❏	❏
8. Are appropriate student behaviors shared with parents in order for them to be reinforced?	❏	❏
9. Is there a school climate team in place to ensure that a positive, peaceful atmosphere is maintained?	❏	❏
10. Is the school climate team composed of administrators, teachers, parents, students, other school staff and community people?	❏	❏
11. Does the school climate team reflect the ethnic make up of the school/ community?	❏	❏
12. Is there a commitment of all staff to the academic achievement of all students?	❏	❏
13. Is there a sense of family (cohesion) in the school?	❏	❏
14. Are there functions that involve staff, students and community?	❏	❏
15. Is there a consistent effort to recognize students for doing well and an opportunity to celebrate their success?	❏	❏

G. CLASS/SCHOOL CLIMATE Continued

		Yes	No
16.	Is there a systematic process for notifying and congratulating parents on their students' growth, achievement or positive behavior?	❏	❏
17.	Are teachers and administrations sensitive to cultural and ethnic differences?	❏	❏

H. COMMUNITY

1.	Does the school encourage parental involvement in its violence prevention/ intervention programs and issues, both in the home and through an organized group (i.e., PTO)?	❏	❏
2.	Do parents receive information on the importance of the home environment and parental role modeling in preventing violent acts?	❏	❏
3.	Is the community population stable and does it have a low transition rate?	❏	❏
4.	Does the community have a low crime rate?	❏	❏
5.	Is there community support for families and children?	❏	❏
6.	Does the community support no use of alcohol and other drugs by minors?	❏	❏
7.	Is there community support for recreational activities for youths after school and during the summer?	❏	❏
8.	Do churches take an active role in providing leadership in violence prevention for youth and families?	❏	❏
9.	Does the community value non-violent behaviors as evidenced by setting and enforcing conservative norms?	❏	❏
10.	Are laws enforced fairly and equitably as they relate to violence?	❏	❏
11.	Does the community support violence prevention/intervention programs, activities and other efforts through its human and financial resources?	❏	❏
12.	Does the community support the school's efforts in the prevention of violence?	❏	❏

I. EVALUATION

		Yes	No
1.	Is research conducted on violence and violent acts of students to establish baseline data and monitor change?	❑	❑
2.	Does the research address specific subcultures (gangs, age and gender).	❑	❑
3.	Is the effectiveness of staff training evaluated on a regular basis?	❑	❑
4.	Are the outcomes of the safe school plan congruent with curriculum and delivery of instruction?	❑	❑
5.	Is data collected that documents prevention and intervention services?	❑	❑

What Can Schools Do?

YOUNG AMERICANS ARE KILLING ONE ANOTHER IN UNPRECEDENTED NUMBERS. Even if our life has not been touched by violence, chances are that it could be. So what can we do?

SUGGESTIONS FROM THE EXPERTS

A.   Dr. Deborah Prothrow-Stith

We can change the climate of violence in our schools. What is required is a broad array of strategies. According to Dr. Prothrow-Stith, a number of factors keep some schools from being swept up in the tide of violence. Research shows that schools that are "safe" have :

- strong principals;
- schools that are not too large;
- schools where discipline is fair, but firm;
- schools where teachers are involved with high expectations for every child;
- schools where parents are drawn into the educational orbit.

Dr. Prothrow-Stith further stresses that the quality of education is a critical factor. Kids who succeed in school are less likely to do drugs, join gangs, or commit violent acts. Schools can prevent violence by insuring that all children are well served academically and by teaching children to manage conflict and anger. Some suggested strategies are:

- implement multi-cultural curricula;
- involve community agencies and law enforcement in school partnerships;
- enforce discipline policies consistently and fairly;
- show concern and interest in students;
- improve both internal and external communication;
- teach conflict resolution, problem solving and crisis intervention skills to students and school staff;
- hire more counselors, social workers and pupil personnel service staff;
- teach discipline, respect, values and responsibility;
- increase parental involvement;
- educate parents about school violence issues;
- offer students peer tutoring, peer counseling and support;

B. **American Medical Association Auxiliary, Inc.**, The Chemical People
Newsletter, Spring 1993

- developing programs to make people aware of the incidence of family violence and how they can be involved in prevention and in support of victims;
- developing programs to make people aware of the problem in their local communities and what they can do to help prevent the problem;
- developing programs for school personnel on the signs of family violence in children and how they can help the victims;
- sponsoring programs for children to make them aware of sexual abuse.

In addition to these strategies, schools may:
- prepare staff to consistently recognize and reward positive youth behavior when it occurs;
- adversatively correct negative behaviors when necessary;
- proactively teach the youth pro-social skills for healthy family and community life; and
- intervene in crises in ways that are non-punitive and mindful of the youth's legal rights.

C. **American Psychological Association**, 1993

- early intervention;
- education program to reduce prejudice and hostility;
- additional services for young perpetrators, victims and witnesses of violence;
- safe school environment;
- early and consistent prevention programs;
- secondary prevention programs that focus on improving individual affective, cognitive and behavioral skills;
- critical viewing skills for analyzing violence in the media;
- utilization of theory and research based approaches to prevention/intervention programming;
- prevention/intervention efforts focused at key times (i.e., school transitions such as, elementary and middle school and key developmental stages such as the beginning of adolescence).

Staff Development

Staff who have the most contact with children usually have the least training and experience in dealing with aggressive and violent youths. Many front line staff have little preparation or have not been prepared to deal adequately with these behaviors.

The better trained a school's staff, the better they will be able to meet the needs of at-risk youths. Some suggested trainings for staff include:

- awareness of the problem at local, state and national levels;
- multi-cultural sensitivity and awareness;
- conflict management and resolution;
- listening and other counseling skills;
- classroom management and discipline;
- mediation;
- reality-based experiences in a variety of school settings/grade levels;
- school/classroom management skills;
- instructional strategies for working with disruptive students;
- communication, human relations and interpersonal skills;
- school violence prevention/intervention programs; and,
- ongoing, updated trainings.

Teachers should be trained to make subject matter relevant to student experiences. Life skills, problem solving, ethnic sensitivity and personal responsibility can be integrated into regular academic curricula. An administrator's best weapons against school violence are organizational, relational and communication skills that inspire teamwork toward clearly defined goals.

Violence Prevention Curricula

Schools can help to shape behaviors and instill pro-social values in the lives of youth when they are provided with appropriate peace keeping skills.

Laying the groundwork for the prevention of violence begins early in a child's development. Children can learn at an early age how to deal with social conflict without resorting to physical and verbal abuse.

There is an abundance of materials masquerading as violence prevention curricula. The quality and effectiveness of these materials should be carefully examined. Beware of vendors that promote materials that promise to have easy solutions to more complicated social problems. Curricula choices need to be based on sound research and theory.

General Curriculum Checklist

The curriculum materials are an important element in the overall effectiveness of the curriculum. The following is a list of basic criteria which should be met. Place a check beside the criteria which characterize the curriculum.

General

_____ Contains a clearly stated, nonviolent, nonaggression philosophy

_____ Supports a total peaceful approach to resolving conflict

_____ Demonstrates respect for the laws and values of society

_____ Promotes healthy, safe and responsible attitudes and behavior both in and out of the school environment

_____ Includes strategies to involve parents, family members and the community in of the school environment the effort to prevent intervention of violence among youth

_____ Contains multiple programming for targeted or diverse populations

_____ Centers around grade specific goals and objectives which have been developed using a sound theoretical/research base

_____ Establish goals and objectives which are realistically attainable and satisfies the needs identified by the local school system

_____ Contains learning objectives which are well-defined, behavioral and measurable and includes both long-term and short-term outcomes

_____ Includes both cognitive and experiential learning objectives

_____ Contains activities which have been designed to meet the objectives

_____ Is grade and age appropriate

_____ Is capable of being integrated into a variety of subject areas

_____ Includes self-control motivations

_____ Contains information on normative beliefs

_____ Current (published or revised within the last three years)

_____ Free from cultural, ethnic, and sexual bias; however, includes cultural, racial, sexual variations as appropriate

_____ Teacher friendly

_____ Durable and safe

_____ Bibliography

_____ Transportable

_____ Reproducible masters (when appropriate)

Violence Specific Information

_____ Contains violence prevention that is current, factual and accurate

_____ Contains appropriate intervention and resource information -- such as referral sources both within the school or the community

_____ Presents a clear and consistent message that the use of verbal and physical abuse is prohibited and is unhealthy and harmful

_____ Incorporates information that explores ways that each individual is unique and valued and has an important role in society

_____ Focuses on the social consequences of violence and the effect it has on the individual and society

_____ Builds an awareness and resistance to influences (family, peer, community and media) which encourage violent use

_____ Print and video materials are based on positive peacekeeping skills as opposed to emphasizing violence

Instructional Strategies and Methodologies

Research findings show that a variety of instructional methods to accommodate different learning styles provide for a more effective curriculum. Using the checklist provided below, determine the types of instructional methods used in the curriculum.

The curriculum includes:

_____ A variety of instructional methods

_____ Cooperative learning

_____ Addresses learning styles

_____ Service learning

_____ Peer Helping

_____ Cross-Age

_____ Diads

_____ Role Playing

_____ Socratic instruction (questioning)

_____ Small group interaction

_____ Large

_____ Teach back (teaching others what they have learned)

Curriculum Content

Contains skill building exercises in the following areas:

_____ Focus of control

_____ Self concept

_____ Problem solving

_____ Healthy relationships

_____ Conflict resolution

_____ Communication and refusal

_____ Negotiation

_____ Decision making

_____ Critical thinking

_____ Coping with stress

_____ Anger management

_____ Skills that build character

_____ Addresses good citizenship

_____ Conservation norm setting

_____ Risk assessment

_____ Social perspective

_____ Peer leadership

_____ Connections between drugs and violence

_____ Team building

_____ Skill rehearsal

_____ Goal setting

_____ Process experiences

_____ Skills evaluation

_____ Sharing and relationship building

_____ Awareness/resistance to pro-violent messages (media, music and etc.)

_____ Identifies positive support system (to include adults outside family)

_____ Knowledge of laws and policies

_____ Involvement in pro-social activities

_____ Address consequence of inappropriate behavior

Commitment to Time

Does the curriculum package include: (check if present)

____ Sufficient time for the objectives to be met

____ Time frames for implementation

____ Time frames for teacher training and ongoing staff development

____ Time frames for preparation

Local Education Agency Specific Criteria

Identifying and matching district specific criteria with the curriculum allows for greater likelihood of success. This list is not comprehensive; it is a starting point for the curriculum evaluation team. There are undoubtedly many other factors that can and should be identified. Use the blank lines provided on the next page to include any additional criteria which have been identified as needs in your community. Place a check beside specific criteria which characterize the curriculum.

____ Does it include materials that are relevant to ethnic groups represented in the district?

____ Does the cost of the curriculum fit within the funds available?

____ Does the curriculum provide for annual content evaluation?

____ Does the curriculum match the time frame available for implementation?

____ Will teachers receive training relevant to the curriculum?

____ Has the curriculum been evaluated on a readability scale and is it grade appropriate?

Additional Local Education Agency specific criteria:

_____

_____

_____

_____

_____

_____

_____

_____

_____

_____

_____

_____

_____

_____

_____

Program Evaluation

_____ The program incorporates a sound curriculum that meets the selection criteria.

_____ The evaluation is clearly linked to program objectives.

_____ The evaluation shows evidence of changes in attitudes, behaviors, and beliefs towards violence and aggression.

_____ The evaluation shows evidence of reduction in aggressive and violent behaviors records collection.

_____ The program provides for an ongoing evaluation.

_____ The program incorporates a sound curriculum that meets the selection criteria.
- *Interviews*
- *Records collections*

Suggestions for curriculum:
- *Pre- and post-test*
- *Portfolios*
- *Journals (notebook entries)*
- *Self assessment*
- *Objective test*

The Importance of Consequences*:

Helping Students Learn From Their Experiences

We have all heard that experience is the best teacher. We often fret over the observation that we cannot simply pass on our wisdom to youth, and that youth seem to have to make their own mistakes. Thus, the importance of consequences. If youth must learn, we can at least make learning more consistent and apparent. Following are some thought provoking questions about consequences.

1. Quickly write down the emotions that come to mind when you hear the work "consequences".

2. Write 5 consequences that increase in seriousness from mild to severe.

3. Define the word "consequence"

4. What are the purposes of consequences?

*Webster: "That which logically or naturally follows from an action or condition: effect."

What Are the Intended Effects of a Consequence?

- To punish the individual for a behavior.

- To make reoccurrence of the behavior by the individual less likely.

- To make the undesired behavior less attractive to others so that they are less likely to engage in the behavior.

- To give the offender an opportunity to make up for the offense.

- To teach the offender more acceptable behavior.

- To strengthen the commitment of the offending individual to understanding and accepting the desired behavior.

- Other?

In implementing a consequence you do not want to so alienate the offending individual so that he/she is unwilling or unlikely to behave more appropriately in the future. You need to build understanding, to handle the consequence fairly, to ensure that all members of the groups' interests are being supported, even the offending member.

In our democratic, capitalist society there is always a tension between the rights and interests of the individual vs. the rights and interests of others. We emphasize individualism, yet pride ourselves on being the "melting pot," where we are able to pull together our collective abilities and forge a better country for all. So, one ultimate purpose of education should be to help individuals develop the skills and behaviors necessary for both their own growth and satisfaction and the benefit of others. We implement both sanctions and training in order to accomplish this.

Reflect on:

1. A time when you were given consequences that you felt were fair. What contributed to the sense of fairness?

2. A time when you were given consequences that you felt were unfair. What contributed to the sense of unfairness?

A "Baker's Dozen"

Suggestions for
Determining and Implementing Consequences

1. In your decision making, explore with the offending individual the purpose of their behavior.

2. As you listen, be careful not to reject out-of-hand the individual's perspective - remember, "perception is reality," and "hearing" the individual's viewpoint may build trust.

3. As you respond, keep in mind certain principles, such as running a school where everyone has a chance to learn and feel safe, and emphasizing the importance of all members, including the offending person, to the group.

4. Ask the offending individual what they think may be an appropriate consequence.

5. If you identify the motivation of the individual, and it can be considered appropriate, try to come up with a more acceptable behavior for the next time the issue occurs.

6. Assign a group of students the task of identifying a range of consequences for certain offenses - benefit from the importance of peer approval, especially among adolescents.

7. In examining the problem behavior, identify those who have been injured, wronged, or inconvenienced. Focus on the interpersonal difficulty created by the behavior.

8. Make sure that the consequence provides an opportunity to make up to individuals who have been wronged.

9. In certain situations it is helpful for the person implementing the consequence to work alongside the person who is being punished. This provides a unique opportunity to build bridges, to improve a relationship that may be influential in future issues.

10. Stay on top of implementing the consequence - see that everything decided is followed up on.

11. When the consequence has been implemented, help the individual move forward by emphasizing that, "the debt has been paid."

12. As much as you can, involve the offending individual in determining a consequence, implementing the consequence, and assessing the results of the consequence; the best goal is an individual who has the skills and desire necessary to maintain appropriate behavior.

13. Show interest in the offending individual aside from the interactions related to the misbehavior.

Activity: **Brainstorm 5 consequences that adhere to the ideas above:**

1.

2.

3.

4.

5.

Safety Enhancement Strategies:
Control Measures

1. Physical Resources

Security Personnel

Generally, every school has at least one individual who has the responsibility of roaming the campus to monitor operations and ensure that no dangerous situations exist. This may be a campus monitor, an assistant principal, or other staff with this specific responsibility. Other individuals who move about campus should also be asked to watch for potentially dangerous or violent situations. For example, custodial staff typically are discretely moving about the building and grounds all day (even before and after normal operating hours). They should be advised to take notice of any unusual activity and to contact the administration immediately.

It is highly advisable that individuals who have the monitoring role be trained in crisis management, specifically including crisis de-escalation techniques. The typical, sometimes authoritarian, techniques that may work with most students, are likely to cause an escalating situation or individual to get worse.

Metal Detectors

Many schools are exploring the use of both walk through and hand-held metal detectors. The experts in this field stress that metal detectors can be part of an overall system of security measures. It is recognized that 100% screening of all students at all times would be expensive and very difficult to accomplish; the time necessary for total searches would greatly interfere with the school's instructional schedule. However, random searches can accomplish much by serving as a deterrent; when students don't know when or where searches are going to occur, many opt not to risk being caught.

Some school systems have chosen to provide hand-held scanners for each school, while having a limited number of walk-through scanners that are randomly moved from school to school (most walk-through equipment is easily portable). This plan allows a school to implement a random search profile, including hand-held and, on occasion, full searches with walk-through equipment.

Regarding costs, a general figure for hand-held equipment is around $300 per unit, while walk-through models are in the range of $3500.

Other Safety Equipment

Communication is a primary need in the event of a dangerous or violent situation on campus. Adequate equipment for routine as well as emergency communications should be available. The most common equipment is the telephone. Walkie-talkies should be available for individuals who supervise the grounds or distant parts of the campus.

Intercoms are useful to communicate directly between the office and classrooms. Emergency call buttons are also useful for classrooms. Beepers and cellular phones are helpful when an individual must be available at all times. Bullhorns and megaphones are useful in dealing with crowds.

Another equipment need is to make sure that adequate first aid supplies are on hand. With heightened awareness of blood-born pathogens, supplies to ensure the safety of individuals who assist the injured are critical. All first aid equipment should be regularly inspected to make sure that it is available and in good condition.

School Building And Grounds

Most schools were not built with security issues as a primary design criteria. Unfortunately, there are many places where violent individuals may hide, and areas of campus where supervision of students is difficult. The areas surrounding a school may present safety issues, as in the urban school that is surrounded by areas known for drug dealing or gang activity.

Supervision and access to assistance are the two major safety issues in dealing with the layout of a school and campus. The campus and surrounding areas should be assessed to determine safe pathways, dangerous areas to be avoided, and lighting needs. It may be helpful to lock selected exterior doors from the outside unless they are needed by students and staff who will be coming in and out of the building via that egress. All areas of campus should be able to be visually supervised, particularly during routine transition periods (e.g., when classes change). This may mean that staff be assigned to position themselves at specific locations to compensate for the layout of the floorplan. Efforts should be made to ensure that no staff or student is routinely assigned to an area that is isolated. Fences and driveway barriers can be useful to control areas where outsiders come onto campus.

In establishing a campus safety layout plan, the intent is not to create a "fortress" where students and staff feel locked in; rather, it is important to have a learning environment with appropriate supervision and freedom from distractions that impede learning. Consideration should be given to the attitude and public profile of campus monitors, as well as the appearance of fences and barriers.

2. Safety-Related Policies

Transition Times And Supervision

Most incidents of student acting-out behavior occur during "between" times -- times when students are moving from one place to another, when lunch is over and they have a few minutes before the next class, on the way to the bus, and before and after school. To minimize all kinds of problems, including violence, keep transition/down times to necessary minimums, and make sure that supervision is available at those times.

For example, it is good to allow students unstructured time after lunch; it is smart to make sure that the students are being supervised by a staff member, that the staff member is close enough to them to enforce campus rules, to be available in case a student steps out of line. As another example, the school should make sure that students arriving early in the morning are supervised; parents should be aware of the earliest time in which children may be left at school.

When students are moving about the building during class periods, hall passes should be required. Staff who allow the movement, as well as staff who receive the student, should sign the pass. It should be clear that a student has permission when she or he is out of class during regular periods.

Visitor Identification Plan

Visitors to a campus should be closely monitored. The vast majority of visitors to a campus are appropriate and well-intentioned; however, it only takes one who is not to create a dangerous situation.

On September 26, 1988, an individual casually walked into Oakland Elementary School in Greenwood, South Carolina, waving to the custodian as he entered, and proceeded to shoot staff members and students. Two students were killed, and two staff members and seven other students were injured.

Immediately after this well-publicized incident, many schools adopted, or began to enforce, visitor identification plans. Unfortunately, as time goes by, schools begin to relax, and enforcement of such policies becomes lax. While it is unhealthy to develop a "siege" mentality, it is prudent to consistently enforce a visitor identification plan. This plan should include:

1. Signs should be posted on all entry doors stating that visitors must report first to the office;

2. After school staff have determined that the individual's business in the school is legitimate, a visitors pass should be given;

3. All school staff members should be instructed to, when they see someone in the school they do not recognize as a part of the school staff, stop, and assertively (though pleasantly) ask if they may help the person. If the person has not already been to the office for a pass, they should be directed to do so;

4. Visitors should be instructed to sign out at the office, returning their pass, when their business is completed.

A school should encourage parents and other appropriate individuals to visit. When a visitor identification policy is warmly, but consistently enforced, the community gets the message that the school prioritizes safety for its students and staff.

School Wide Crisis-Management Plan - Every school should have a plan in place to deal with emergency situations. Whether it is a willful incident of violence within the school, an act of nature, or a fire that breaks out, the school needs to have a plan for dealing with the needs of students, staff, and families. This plan should include the following elements:

1. **Appropriate emergency information readily available for students and staff, including telephone numbers, emergency contacts, special medication needs, or skills** of staff members that may be useful in emergencies (e.g., CPR training).

2. **A clear communication plan** - who is to be notified, who does the contacting, what should students be told, what documentation should occur, who is in charge.

3. **Identified pathways/safe areas/door locking procedures** for the school building and grounds. For example, for fire drills there is a plan that includes where students and staff go, who clears the building, what people do while awaiting the all clear signal, etc. A similar plan for incidents of violence is important. When a dangerous individual is on campus, there should be a way to notify staff. Staff should know what action(s) should be taken (locking doors, turning out lights, etc.).

It would be advisable for each school to rehearse its general emergency plan just as it does for fire emergencies. When people are in the middle of a crisis, they tend to act on instinct. Practicing in advance increases the likelihood that you will remember the emergency procedures.

4. **Readily available numbers to call for off campus assistance and notification** should be on hand. How do you contact the police? Who should make that contact? Who needs to be notified of the contact? For example, in some districts the principal is authorized to contact local police. A call must immediately be placed to the superintendent's office, as calls from the media (who monitor police radio contacts) and parents will be coming in. To assist in maintaining calm at emergency times it is critical to inform appropriate individuals.

There are many other details that should be considered in developing a thorough crisis management plan. An excellent resource is <u>Containing Crisis - A Guide to Managing School Emergencies</u>, by Watson, et.al., 1990.

School Policies On Aggressive/Abusive Management Of Students

If schools are intent on teaching nonviolence to students, it is critical that staff members work with students in nonviolent ways. Verbal and physical intimidation and excessive physical management have no place in a program that deals with children and youth. If such techniques are used, the students get the message that violence is an acceptable way to resolve problems. It is strongly suggested that training be available to assist staff members in developing management skills that are nonviolent.

Note that, aside from the specific issue of corporal punishment, schools do not advocate violence for student management. However, while schools generally have specific policies on how to report suspected abuse of students by family members, the policies relating to suspected abuse by school staff are frequently very general. It is recommended that districts and schools develop policies regarding verbal and physical abuse of students, including the issue of physical intervention.

3. Social/Emotional Climate Enhancement

Everyone wants to spend their time in settings that are, at a minimum, physically and psychologically safe. Physical safety entails the obvious; we do not want to be hurt, we do not want to be victimized, we do not want to be physically endangered.

Psychological safety, on the other hand, is much more difficult to identify. It is not as directly visible, the impact is sometimes long in coming. Psychological safety is more like a slow simmer, whereas physical safety is like charring on the grill. Psychological safety is not being abused, ridiculed, overly chastised, abandoned or rejected, labeled a failure, or judged to be hopeless. It means not being treated with indifference.

Beyond the base level of safety, human beings need to be surrounded by a social and emotional climate that encourages physical and psychological growth. Such a setting encourages the individual to grow in his/her relationships, in cognitive and mental skills, in academic abilities, and in self-esteem. It nurtures the individual's personality and allows growth in all areas of human functioning.

The American Psychological Association, in a report entitled <u>Violence and Youth: Psychology's Response</u> (1993), suggests that the following are factors that increase the likelihood of violence:

1. A fearless and impulsive temperament early in life may show a propensity for violent and aggressive behavior;

2. A breakdown of family processes and relationships may contribute to the development of antisocial behaviors;

3. Harsh and continual punishment by parents is associated with the development of aggressive behavior patterns.

4. Exposure to high levels of violence in the media may contribute to more aggressive behaviors.

Reading between the lines of this report, one finds support for the need to provide a life setting that is physically and psychologically safe, one with a positive and nurturing social and emotional climate.

How do we provide such a setting in schools?

Richard Curwin, in an article entitled "Helping Students Rediscover Hope" (The Journal of Emotional and Behavioral Problems, Spring, 1994, pp.27-30), identifies 10 aspects of a classroom or school that contribute to positive growth and functioning:

1. Students accurately believe that they are competent in the subjects they are learning. They reach at least one meaningful goal each day.

2. Learning tasks that are not too easy.

3. The information being taught is meaningful to the students, and is congruent with their values.

4. The learning process is active; students are involved in a variety of learning activities.

5. Teachers show their genuine energy and love for teaching.

6. Students perceive that classroom goals and activities are real and not simply gimmicks; the students feel that what they are learning is important and useful.

7. Learning is fun and enjoyable.

8. Students feel that they are wanted and welcomed in their classrooms and school.

9. The student feels that at least one teacher or adult makes a personal connection to him/her.

10. Teachers plan to make their instruction motivating.

Larry Brendtro, Martin Brokenleg, and Steve Van Bockern look at this issue from the perspective of Native American child-rearing values. In The Circle of Courage (Beyond Behavior, Winter, 1991, pp. 5 - 12), the authors suggest that families and communities (including schools) should seek four areas of development for children:

1. All children need to have a sense of belonging, that they are an important part of a family, a school, a community.

2. All children need to develop a sense of competence, of mastery of their environments.

3. Children need to become independent, but in the context of an understanding that they are an integral part of the community.

4. All children need to experience generosity, the feeling of giving to and being needed by others.

4. Other Resources

Student and staff safety may also be enhanced by looking to the community for additional support.

School Advisory Committee
Generally the school has committees in place whose members include school staff and parents. Some advisory committees also include community representatives. Depending on the demographics, neighborhood, and community you may want to include a representative from the police department, the courts, a juvenile judge, mental health programs, social service programs, etc. These representatives would then have an inside line to begin to understand the issues with which schools must deal. Through ongoing dialogue, additional solutions to have an impact on violence may develop.

Community Based Programs

It has been said that violence is not a school problem -- it is a community problem. Effective efforts to reduce violence must be waged by the schools, families, and communities. An effective long-term effort to reduce violence is going to require a gradual whittling away, an eroding of the factors that encourage violence, as well as a creation of the factors that decrease violence.

What can be done community-wide to reduce violence? Following are some of the activities that are being implemented, as well as some that could be tried.

1. After school tutorial programs - Provides structured time as well as academic assistance to help students be successful in school.

2. After school recreational programs - Provides structured activities under the supervision of adults; a well known example is the "Midnight Hoops" program which has established basketball teams and sets up games in community recreation sites. The games are often played late in the evenings and at night, during the time frames which are high risk for students getting involved in negative behaviors.

3. Conflict management training programs - Provides training to interested individuals in the community on how to resolve conflicts peacefully. These programs are similar to those provided in some schools, emphasizing the fact that conflict is natural, and teaching people skills to successfully deal with conflict. Churches and other community organizations have served as bases for this type of training.

4. Mentoring programs - Students who grow up in single parent homes are particularly at risk for negative behaviors, including violence. Mentoring programs match an individual student with an interested adult who seeks to develop a positive relationship with the student.

5. Positive Rites of Passage programs - What are the rights of passage in our culture? How do children know that they are becoming adults? What experiences serve as recognition that a child has become an adult? There are some who feel that the primary "rites of passage" into adulthood are the incidents when youth engage in activities that are thought of as adult activities. Many of these activities are detrimental to the child (and often to the adult, as well). For example, sexual experiences or use of drugs, including tobacco, alcohol, and illicit drugs. Recently, in a report on National Public Radio, a youth was quoted as saying that going to prison has its advantages. When you return to the community you are given "respect" for having handled the prison experience. Unfortunately, this avenue to "respect" encourages the use of violence.

As an example of a positive rite of passage program, "Manhood Training: An Introduction to Adulthood for Inner City Boys Ages 11 to 13" was developed by Professor O'Neal Smalls of the University of South Carolina. The purpose of the training is to provide boys between the ages of 11 and 13 with experiences and training that help them develop a sense of social, group, and personal responsibility and respect. The activities include specific training as well as rituals to symbolize movement into manhood.

Parent Involvement

Connecting with parents is critical and essential in order to have an effective school. The common interest in the health and well-being of the child/student from parents and school staff should act as a bond creating a circle of support on behalf of the young person. However, this is not always the case. Often schools complain that parents don't care and they are not available when needed to discuss issues/concerns relating to their child. The fact is many parents have had bad experiences in school and find schools to be cold institutions that are patronizing and unwelcoming. Joining with parents in a manner that allows for dialogue and mutual concern must become a top priority as we look toward quality education in the twenty-first century.

Schools join with parents when:

1. Teachers call or write parents to affirm the positive qualities, talents and attributes of their child.

2. Parents are treated as experts on their children.

3. Parents are solicited for help and advice regarding student behavior or performance.

4. Parents are not outnumbered at parents/teacher conferences.

5. Personnel considers alternative meeting sites other than school.

6. Parents are welcomed into the school and classroom.

7. Parents are viewed as advocates and allies as opposed to "the enemy."

8. Parents are recruited to serve on the advisory committee for the school.

9. Parents are informed in writing and verbally of the school and classroom rules and are aware of consequences related to rule violation.

10. Parents are offered support groups and parent education classes.

11. Single parents are supported.

12. The school is promoted and viewed as a "community school."

13. Parents are treated respectfully from support personnel to administration.

14. Parents are asked to volunteer for functions, etc.

15. Parents are invited to the school to celebrate or eat lunch with their child(ren).

Levels of Aggression/Precursors to Violence

Aggression: Initiation of forceful, usually hostile,
action against another (*Webster, 1984*).

Prevention and Proactive Training

"You can pay me now, or you can pay me later""...How many times have we heard that truism? Following is a rather complex graph suggesting different types of aggression, and proposing different ways to respond proactively. Study each dimension and see if you are able to identify where students you are concerned about may fit. Then put together your own proactive training plan to help the students develop the skills necessary to minimize violence and aggression in his/her (and your!) life.

Dimensions of Aggression (Dimension 1)

TYPE	BASELINE BEHAVIOR	PRECIPITANT	COGNITIVE FUNCTION	DESCRIPTION OF ACT	RESPONSE	INTER-VENTION

Over Aroused "Tornado"	• High level activity/hyperactive
	• Often provoke or initiate aggressive response
	• Excessive arousal
		• Trivial, incidental inconveniences or limits
		• Whatever gets in the way
			• Misinterpret social cues and behaviors of others
			• Object of their explosiveness
			• Unplanned selected incidental
			• Little preoccupation or intentionality
				• Moderate intensity and duration
				• Rarely intend to do harm
				• Bring a lot of energy to aggression
				• Use of weapon usually incidental
				• Want to reduce external demands and external resistance
					• Often embarrassed by their behavior
					• May apologize
					• Remorse seldom prevents future aggression
					• Their high drive state seldom allows stop and think behavior
						• Reduce excessive stimulation in environment
						• Provide alternatives for excess energy
						• Relazation training
						• Solical siklls training: especially
						  * negotiation
						  * problem solving
						  * communication skills

Dimensions of Aggression (Dimension 2)

TYPE	BASELINE BEHAVIOR	PRECIPITANT	COGNITIVE FUNCTION	DESCRIPTION OF ACT	RESPONSE	INTER-VENTION
Impulsive "Reptilian" Aggression	• Characterized by sudden burst of violence • May be passive/lethargic • Low tolerance for frustration • Often irritable • Easily upset • Rarely satisfied or joyful • Often seen in organically impaired child and attention deficit disorder	• Minimal frustration or inconveniences • Accidental shove • Minimal restriction • Moderate irritation	• Often cognitively impaired • Response is rapid, impulsive, unselective • Little attention paid to who is struck or hurt • May hurt those they like or love • Can't/don't analyze situation	• Temper tantrum • Easily redirected or consoled • Oblivious to harm they have done • Attacks are generally brief in duration but of high intensity • May rage instantly over minimal incident	• Sometimes "surprised" by own outburst • May explain-- "I lost my temper" • Have no knowledge of effect their behavior has on others • Surprised by withdrawal and rejection resulting from their behavior • Incident when over is quickly forgotten by	these youth

Dimensions of Aggression (Dimension 3)

TYPE	BASELINE BEHAVIOR	PRECIPITANT	COGNITIVE FUNCTION	DESCRIPTION OF ACT	RESPONSE	INTERVENTION
Affective Aggression "Raging Bull"	• May appear chronically angry, resentful, hostile • May be irritable and dissatisfied • May expect to be harmed	• May have been abused • May have witnessed violence • Anger may be rooted in chronic abuse coupled with helplessness • Sometimes wished to defend selves and/or family from violence • Now looking to defend selves often from situations that pose no threat	• May expect abuse because of past abuse • Incidents, accidents perceived as hostile or menacing • May be deliberate and plot their aggression or exhibit visually unprovoked rage	• Notable degree of rage, affect and energy • Rage doesn't end easily • Power of rage rooted in wrongs of childhood not event of the moment • Violence may be prolonged, intense goal directed and dangerous • Object of violence may be a hopeless person who reminds student of past	• youth will likely blame the victim • "It's his fault I'm angry" (based on a minor justification) • With some insight may acknowledge he/she can't control his/her temper	• Social skill development needed • Conflict resolution skills • May benefit from group counseling • May need to be referred for therapy

Dimensions of Aggression (Dimension 4)

TYPE	BASELINE BEHAVIOR	PRECIPITANT	COGNITIVE FUNCTION	DESCRIPTION OF ACT	RESPONSE	INTER-VENTION
Predatory Aggression "Stalking Lion"	• Processes aggression with control and deliberation • Often plans, waits for their chance and the right opportunity	• Precipitant often rooted in behavior that was considered demeaning, insulting or harmful	• Preoccupied with getting even • Vigilant in looking for possible insults, possible harm or danger • May over interpret potential danger in precipitating events • May seem paranoid in expectation of events	• Aggression often planned secretive and vindictive • Usually care fully chooses the object of aggression • May stalk or pursue • Aggression may be brief and affect less • Executed with joyful glee • Passive aggressive behavior	• Reflects on behavior with pride • May claim justice • "I don't get mad, I get even."	• Needs alternative non-aggressive social skills and socialization • Integrate to pro-social peer groups • Conflict resolution training • Find other ways of meeting power needs and achieving rewards

Dimensions of Aggression (Dimension 5)

TYPE	BASELINE BEHAVIOR	PRECIPITANT	COGNITIVE FUNCTION	DESCRIPTION OF ACT	RESPONSE	INTER-VENTION
Instrumental Aggression "Intimidating Bully"	• Uses aggression to get his/her way • Winning through intimidation • Extreme cases of sociopath • Energetic and ambitious but <u>not</u> hyperactive • May come from violent, antisocial environment	• Possibly had a childhood of violence, deviance when antisocial behavior rewarded • Precipitant may be minimal in sult, gesture defiance that precipitates a need to establish dominance	• Cognitively intact • Aggression intentional, planned, strategic • May use intimidation and threats (direct or indirect to gain and consolidate power	• Duration depends on "political" purpose from speed of a snake to slow wearing down of opposition • Act is controlled, not accidental • Object of aggression often a competitor or offender	• Often displays pride in aggression • Rarely blames self rather congratulates self	• Social skills training to increase conflict resolution abilities • Rewards for legitimate achievement • May increase or desire an incentive for pro-social behavior • Interpersonal intervention often

Adapted from *Neurological Patterns of Aggression*, Robert D. Hunt (1993). *Journal of Emotional & Behavioral Problems*, Vol. II, Issue I.

Precursors to Violence
Assessment Instrument

Directions: Read each statement and mark the appropriate response in the corresponding space.

A. PERSONAL (ranked developmentally)

	Yes	No
1. Does the student exhibit a fearless temperament?	❏	❏
2. Does the student exhibit impulsive behavior?	❏	❏
3. Is there evidence of an inability to concentrate?	❏	❏
4. Does the child demonstrate the inability to delay gratification?	❏	❏
5. Is language processing or cognition developmentally impaired?	❏	❏
6. Does the student display daring and risk-taking behaviors?	❏	❏
7. Does the student have a low empathy for others who are victimized?	❏	❏
8. Does the student exhibit a fascination for violence in print and in the media?	❏	❏
9. Is there evidence of early school failure?	❏	❏
10. Does the child exhibit behaviors of a bully?	❏	❏
11. Does the child have pro-social friends?	❏	❏
12. Did student begin the use of alcohol and drugs prior to age 15?	❏	❏
13. Is there a lack of commitment to school?	❏	❏
14. Does the student exhibit cruelty to animals and younger children?	❏	❏
15. Does the child intentionally set fires to property?	❏	❏
16. Does the student exhibit a flat affect?	❏	❏
17. Does the student have a low threshold to frustration?	❏	❏
18. Does the student exhibit outbursts of rage?	❏	❏

B. FAMILY

	Yes	No
1. Does the student come from a violent and abusive family?	❏	❏
2. Has the student ever been neglected or abused?	❏	❏
3. Does the student lack supervision by a parent or an adult at home?	❏	❏
4. Does the family provide harsh or inconsistent discipline?	❏	❏
5. Is there a lack of parental or adult nurturing?	❏	❏

B.   FAMILY Continued

	Yes	No
6. Was the student separated from parent(s) at an early age?	❏	❏
7. Does the student have family members who have been committed for violent or criminal behavior?	❏	❏
8. Does the student have adequate food for daily meals?	❏	❏
9. Does the student have adequate and appropriate clothing?	❏	❏
10. Does the student have adequate and appropriate housing?	❏	❏
11. Is family life-style at or below poverty level?	❏	❏
12. Are there frequent incidences of family conflict?	❏	❏
13. Are there favorable parental attitudes and involvement regarding violent behaviors?	❏	❏

C.   COMMUNITY

	Yes	No
1. Is the student's home located in a high crime neighborhood?	❏	❏
2. Is there an availability of drugs and firearms?	❏	❏
3. Are the community laws and norms favorable towards drug use, firearms and crime?	❏	❏
4. Is there low neighborhood attachment and community disorganization?	❏	❏
5. Is there extreme economic and social deprivation?	❏	❏

"No one thinks clearly when his fists are clenched."

George Jean Nathan

"Anger is one letter away from danger."

Anonymous

"Not the cry, but the flight of the wild duck, leads the flock to fly and follow."

Chinese Proverb

Section III:

6

Powerful Skills for Managing & Surviving Hostile or Aggressive Students

Is there a Lone Ranger?
Seeking the Magic Bullet...

Unfortunately there is no magic bullet, but there is a bag of tricks ant you can draw upon. Following are six powerful skills that will help you prevent problems from beginning, de-escalate situations that are on the rise, and learn from problems that have occurred. These thoughtful techniques will equip you with knowledge to handle complex traps and games!

Skill #1 - Mine Sweeping

The image of a mine sweeper is that of an individual extending an instrument ahead of himself to check for mines instead of just stepping blindly on them and experiencing the consequences.

The "mines" that we wish to avoid are the loaded emotions of an individual who could erupt with aggression or violence. "Mine Sweeping" is searching for the emotions, feelings, motivations, or "red flags" that an individual has which could lead to volatility.

Think of an "emotional mine" that needs to be avoided in an individual you know. How do you avoid that mine?

Skill #2 - De-Fusing

An explanation of defusing is identifying anything in your classroom that leads to or exacerbates aggravations; looking for those simple or complex things that "bug" people so much that they may become irritable or worse; looking for things that could trigger aggression or violence.

Some examples of these triggers could include:
challenging eye contact
space needs/crowding
touch/lack of touch
different learning styles
gender differences
relevance of the material/boredom
rigidity
chaos
judgmental attitude
high criticism/low warmth class
distractibility

What really irritates you in a learning situation?

Think of triggers or irritants that you have observed in your students.

Skill #3 - Unhooking

Though we often bemoan the "lack of social skills" in many of our youth, how often do we find that we have been masterfully manipulated by one of the same? Individuals can have tremendous ability to involve us in their own conflicts, or conflicts with another person, by "hooking" us into a game triangle. We sometimes refer to this experience as:

- rescuing the scapegoat

- having each individual in a conflict - independently - involve us in how unfairly the other individual has treated them

- succumbing to the seduction of being someone's problem solver

- being caught in a grand manipulation

So how do we avoid being "hooked"?

- Set clear expectations early

- Calmly stay with your expectations

- Practice good listening skills with all individuals

- Remember that the shortest path between two objects is usually a straight line; when someone comes to you to rescue them from another's maltreatment, your best bet is to help the individual do their own negotiating, their own problem solving. If you do it for them, you run the risk of becoming part of the problem, and of not teaching the individual so that they will be capable of dealing with similar issues independently.

Think of a time when you were "caught." How did it happen? What characteristic in yourself made you susceptible to being caught? What skill did the individual have that caught you?

Skill #4 - Game-Triangle

The "game-triangle" is a model depicting patterns of interaction that are familiar to "at-risk" students. If they can set up this triangle in an interaction, they may gain a sense of familiarity and power or security over it.

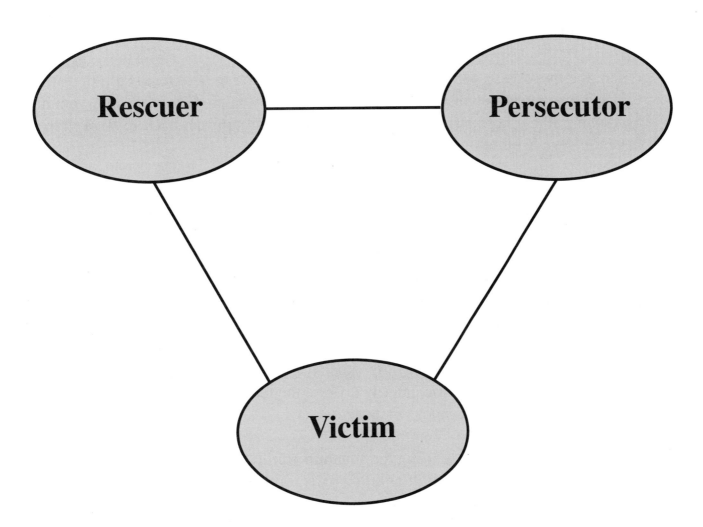

The amount of success one has in working with a hostile/aggressive student depends heavily on the ability he or she has to "unhook" from the "game-triangle."

Skill #5 - De-Escalating

Sometimes you can see one or more individuals beginning to escalate, to loose rationality, behaving as though they do not remember or care about the consequences of their actions. This is the time when you hope to calmly and deliberately do something to calm the situation. De-escalating is the skill of intervening early in an aggressive episode and helping the individuals settle down. It may happen when you have not been effective at "mine-sweeping" or "de-fusing."

Tips and pointers for de-escalation:

- Often, the individuals are hoping that someone is going to help them stop the situation before it gets out of hand. They may secretly appreciate your intervention. Something like a bold statement of, "This is a classroom; get back to work!" may have the desired effect.

- Removal of one party, particularly the aggressor, from the area may be extremely effective. You can innocently request that the individual, "take this message to the office", giving both time to calm down.

- Simple physical proximity of the adult in charge can settle down an escalating situation. Walk calmly and deliberately towards the area of disturbance.

- Distractions - sometimes you can do something completely unrelated to distract the individuals. For example, "accidently" knocking over your chair, or letting the book slip from your hand, may momentarily distract the individuals, giving you an opportunity to reengage them in appropriate activity.

- Humor - you may be able to make the situation a little lighter by use of humor. Caution: do not use humor that belittles either party, or that occurs at someone's expense.

Skill #6 - Psychological Martial Arts

A. How to Handle a Verbal "Attack"

1. **Find out where your opponent's "attack" is coming from.**
   Use Open Questions such as "What" and "How" to explore his or her story and beliefs about the situation. Avoid asking "Why" questions because they may sound blaming.

2. **Study your opponent's power.**
   Use feeling-focused responses to study your opponent's emotions about the situation.

3. **Grab hold of this power, step out of its way, and encourage it to move past you without letting it get to you.**
   Use summarizing responses to keep the focus away from you for a while. This may help diffuse his or her "attack" and help you keep "cool."

4. **If this fails, walk away without saying another word.**
   If you can't walk away, "keep your cool" until you can talk it out with a support person.

B. Three Personal Qualities to Master

Power   Be aware of the potential in your:
- Personal strengths.
- Successes.
- Determination.
- Motivations.
- Resources.

Balance   Work at achieving balance in your life between the:
- Physical,
- Social,
- Emotional,
- Work (school), &
- Spiritual.

Control   Strive to have self-control by:
- Being responsible.
- "Keeping your cool" when provoked.

"Kindness is the oil that takes the friction out of life."

Anonymous

"A bully is always a coward."

Thomas Chandler Haliburton

"If peace is to last, it must come first.."

Anonymous

Section IV:

Classroom Strategies

Recipe for a Peaceful World

Purpose

Become aware of differences that exist in society.
Value and respect differences.
Develop a recipe for peace.
Share activities with someone other than a classmate.

Procedures

1. Divide the class into groups of four.

2. Appoint these roles to each group member: facilitator, recorder, time keeper and reporter.

3. Allow each group 20-25 minutes to develop a recipe (choose one):
    a. world peace
    b. working and playing together
    c. respecting differences in gender, race, religion, culture
    d. respect for diversity in values, opinions, style of dress, etc.

4. Instruct groups to follow the same format as a cooking recipe; for example, 1 lb. of tolerance mixed with 1/2 cup of humor, etc.

5. Recipes are to be written on chart butcher paper, or poster, etc.

6. Each group will present its recipe to the class.

Follow-Up

Have students record in their journals or write a letter to their parents and/or principals regarding the meaning or the impact this activity has on them. Include a paragraph on their hopes and wishes for a peaceful world…

Don't Let Your Anger Balloon

Purpose

To identify angry feelings.
To recognize when our anger starts to swell.
To learn to deflate our anger balloon.
To recognize when our anger balloon may burst.

Procedures

1. Put students into groups of 2-4.

2. Give each student a balloon.

3. Ask students to imagine that a balloon represents their feelings of anger.

4. Ask students what would happen if they kept blowing into the balloon. (It would burst. Demonstrate if you wish.)

5. Ask students to deflate their balloons -- equate to reducing the anger.

Follow-Up

In small groups each will:

1. Identify behaviors or situations that make their anger balloons inflate.

2. Identify behaviors or situations that can help deflate their anger, then deflate their balloons.

3. Identify strategies that they can use to keep their anger balloons from bursting.

4. Develop a class balloon profile for managing anger.

What are the Emotions of Violence?

Reflect for a few moments on an incident of violence that you have experienced.

Briefly describe the incident.

What feelings did you have during the incident?

How did you respond to the individual committing the violence?

What were your greatest fears during the incident?

What did you do immediately after the incident?

Did you find yourself behaving differently afterwards? How?

Did you talk to anyone after the incident? Who?

How long did you think about the incident?

Have there been any lasting changes in your behavior or feelings as a result of the incident?

Violence & Aggression in the Media

Purpose

To increase awareness regarding violence in the media.
To utilize critical thinking skills when
viewing television.

Procedures

1. Hand out student activity sheet on "Violence & Aggression in the Media."

2. Ask students to select and watch any program from the following categories: family show, soap opera, action/drama, cartoon, commercials or MTV and record the number of violent or aggressive behaviors that occurred during the viewing time.

Follow-Up

1. What conclusions can be drawn from this data?

2. What issues and concerns do you have regarding media violence and aggression?

3. What are the values of the message conveyed in the violent and aggressive acts you observed?

4. What if the message implied in the program you viewed occurred consistently in school? your neighborhood? our nation?

5. If these were the only programs that were viewed by foreigners, what conclusions could they draw about our society?

Violence & Aggression in the Media

Select and watch any program from the following categories: family show, soap opera, action/drama, movie, cartoon, commercial, news or MTV and record your results on this chart.

Program 1: _____
(name of program, movie, song, commercial, etc.)

Day and Time Viewed: _____
(day of week/hour a.m. or p.m.)

Types of Violent/Aggressive Acts or Behaviors

	Total Number		Total Number
Guns	_____	Knives	_____
Fists	_____	Hitting	_____
Kicking	_____	Slapping	_____
Biting	_____	Hair Pulling	_____
Burning	_____	Animals	_____
Verbal	_____	Sexual	_____
Racial	_____	Religious	_____
Gender	_____	Power Misuse	_____
Blackmail	_____	Mob/Gang	_____
War	_____	Other	_____

The Great Debate

Purpose

To develop critical thinking skills regarding violence
and aggression in the media.
To develop a rationale and logic for supporting
one's view point

Procedures

1. Divide the class into two groups by asking them to count off 1, 2, 1, 2, etc.

2. Read this statement to the class: "Television and movies <u>do</u> or <u>do not</u> have an impact on young people's behavior."

3. Assign the ones (1's) the pros of television and movies and the two (2's) the cons.

4. Tell the class they will be given ample time to develop their points for discussing their side of the issue.

5. Establish cooperative groups within each large group with designated responsibilities (such as interviews, polls, etc.).

6. Select a debate team from each side consisting of 2-3 members. All other team members will supply their debate team with points for the "great debate."

7. Select a panel of 5 judges. These may be staff, parents or community volunteers.

8. Develop criteria for judging with scoring information.

Follow-Up

1. Have the class develop guidelines for viewing television and movies and share these with: parents, movie production companies and television stations.

2. What recommendations would you make to tv and movie producers regarding what adolescents should view? Explain the rationale for your recommendations.

How Does Violence Affect Others in Your School?

List incidents of violence that adults in your school setting have experienced.

How have these experiences affected the individuals involved?

List incidents of violence that students in your school setting have experienced.

How have these experiences affected the learning environment for students?

A learning setting free from the likelihood of physical or psychological violence should be a given for schools. What is reasonable for a student to expect in terms of an atmosphere conducive to learning?

- A room that can be quiet enough for concentration
- Opportunities to learn from reading, talking, looking, doing
- Comfort that their materials are going to be respected - they will be there when the student needs them
- A sense of physical protection and safety for everyone
- Assurance that trying your best, even if you fail, is good
- Opportunities to learn from failures
- Freedom from psychological harassment
- Encouragement

Reframing: Making Lemonade Out of Lemons

Reframing is predicated on the belief that for most negative words and behaviors there is an underlying positive intent. If educators learn to reframe negative words, phrases and behaviors, they will be able to:

1. See students in a positive light

2. Defuse rather than escalate a potentially negative encounter

3. Absorb a potentially hostile situation rather than responding in kind

Reframing should not be used to replace communication skills such as reflective listening or "I" messages, but as an additional communication tool. Use reframing techniques sparingly and with assurance. Never explain or argue about your reframe. Use it rather to turn the corner or to acknowledge the positive lurking under the hostile or aggressive words.

How does it work? Here are a few examples. Then try it for yourself.

Negative	Reframe
1. Slob	1. Laid back, casual, carefree
2. Domineering	2. Assertive, leader, take-charge person
3. "This group is a waste of time."	3. "It's clear to me that how you spend your time is important to you!"
4. "No matter how hard I try, I'll never be able to understand this stuff."	4. "It's clear to me that doing well and understanding your work is a priority."

Try these:

<u>Negative</u>	<u>Reframe</u>
1. SNOB	_____
2. NERD	_____
3. CONTROLLING	_____
4. FLIGHTY	_____
5. COLD	_____
6. EGOTISTICAL	_____
7. CHICKEN	_____
8. ALOOF	_____
9. BORING	_____
10. HOSTILE	_____

Reframe each of the following statements to become a positive expression.

1. This school sucks!

   _____

2. You never use the rules on anybody else!

   _____

3. Why didn't you make Jane stay after school too?

   _____

4. I'm not the one with the problem, you guys are.

   _____

5. If everyone would just leave me alone, I'd be fine.

   _____

6. It's not my fault, you made me do it.

   _____

7. You told me I could have this hall pass.

   _____

8. The principal's just got it in for me.

   _____

9. This homework is stupid.

   _____

10.   If you give John a "B" on this, then I deserve an "A".

   _____

"I want you to stop the killing in the city...I think that somebody might kill me."

James Darby, April 29, 1994

This quote is from a letter written by James to President Clinton, out of worry over what he had seen happening in his neighborhood, to his friends.

Nine days later, on Mother's Day, 9 year old James Darby was shotgunned to death.
(Bob Herbert, "Children Paying the Price of Crime," article in The State, Columbia, SC, July 21, 1994)

Section V:

Teaching Students the Steps to:

Anger Management & Control

Conflict Resolution

Creative Assertiveness

"Bully Fighting"

Peer Mediation

Teaching Students the Steps to Anger Management and Control

Ways to "Keep Your Cool" When Provoked
(Refusal Skills for Avoiding Losing your Temper)

1. Relaxation Techniques

    a. Self-Talk

    b. Breathing

2. Giving Effective Feedback

    a. Sending

    b. Receiving

3. Creative "Come-Backs"

    a. Psychological Martial Arts (see Section III: Six Powerful Skills for Managing and Surviving Hostile or Aggressive Students)

    b. Humor

    c. Tapping Peer Support

4. Turning Away Without "Losing Face"

5. Obtaining Outside Support

Understanding Anger and Internal Hostility

1. We can learn to "manage our anger" through learning:
   - to understand information about anger and internal hostility in ourselves and others.
   - to use strategies that can prevent or delay our automatic responses to anger.

2. Anger is an inner reaction to outside events and personal experiences.

3. Anger may be measured according to its:
   - intensity
   - duration
   - frequency

4. Anger is a "secondary" emotion which appears after feeling hurt.

5. Different situations evoke and escalate our anger at different
   - rates
   - intensities

6. Anger, when held inside without release, is called "internal hostility." Internal hostility is sometimes hidden from others, but eventually is released:
   - at the true provoker
   - at the environment
   - at others
   - at one's self

7. Internal hostility can build up over time, but it primarily originates from unresolved feelings from:
   - loss
   - victimization (usually from being abused/neglected)

8. Internal hostility may show in:
   - Unusually intense, frequent, or long-lasting expressions of anger
   - Psychosomatic illnesses or depression
   - Projected expressions through
     - games/sports
     - visual art
     - writing/poetry
     - other creative arts
     - music

9. From early childhood, we learn responses to anger that become automatic. These responses are:
    - culturally influenced
    - gender influenced
    - learned from:
        - parents and other family role-models
        - media (for example, movies and video games)
        - peers
        - experimentation

10. We can learn to change our automatic anger responses through:
    a. Understanding anger in ourselves and others:
        - anger origins • "anger sequence" • anger triggers
    b. Practicing different ways to respond to anger
    c. Developing an action plan
    d. Sharing successes

Learning About Your Anger Sequence

1. **What pushes your anger button?**

2. **Why does it push your button?**

3. **How do you respond inside when your anger button is pushed?**
   a. Thoughts—self talk
   b. Feelings/emotional arousal
   c. Psychological arousal

4. **How do you respond outwardly when your anger button is pushed?**

5. **What are the consequences for yourself and other(s) when you "lose your cool" inappropriately?**
   a. Thoughts—appraisals, self-talk
   b. Feelings—e.g., self-worth, depression, guilt, etc.
   c. Behaviors—e.g., avoidance, crying, aggression

Learning Appropriate Anger-Expression Skills

1. **Before your anger is triggered**

    Helpful

    Harmful

2. **When your anger is first triggered**

    Helpful

    Harmful

3. **Once you become very upset**

    Helpful

    Harmful

4. **After the anger dies down**

    Helpful

    Harmful

Conflict Caveats

Conflict is a natural part of life.

Conflict can be dealt with positively or negatively.

Conflict can be constructive or destructive.

Conflict has been and can be a mechanism for personal growth and social change.

Conflict Occurs When

Basic needs are not met.

There is a struggle over power.

There is a struggle over allocation and use of resources.

There are incompatible goals and values.

Conflict Resolution

Conflict is a strong disagreement or collision of values, needs, interests or intentions among individuals, groups, organizations, communities and nations.

Conflict is a natural part of everyday life. It occurs when our basic needs for belonging, power, freedom, or fun are not met. Conflict can either be creative or destructive. It can be a positive force for personal and social growth and change.

Constructive Resolution

Constructive conflicts are beneficial to the intellectual, social and emotional growth of students and will:

1. Promote intellectual development

2. Clarify relationships

3. Clarify values and commitments

4. Provide energy for creating social change (i.e., civil rights movement)

5. Promote human development

6. Promote appreciation of different perspectives

7. Provide pleasure (i.e., sporting events, debates)

8. Provide create insights

9. Provide for negotiation of a solution

10. Provide for options

11. Provide for modification of behavior

12. Provide acceptable outlet for anger

13. Provide mechanisms for appropriate patterned responses

14. Promote open dialogues

15. Promote cooperative efforts

16. Promote collaboration and teaming

17. Promote and enhance peacekeeping skills

Steps to Conflict Resolution Model

1. What's the conflict?

a. Defuse the issue
- Use lots of summarizing responses to help each disputee feel accepted and understood.
- Bring out each person's needs and goals in the situation.

b. Clarify feelings
- Tap the healing power of catharsis (perhaps this is all that is really needed).
- Summarize each side before going to the next step.

2. What have you tried?

What else?

3. What else could you do? What would probably happen if you did that?

Brainstorm alternatives and explore probable consequences.

What would happen if you did nothing?
What would happen if you...? (make suggestions)

4. What's your next (first) step?

When are you going to start? (be specific)

Role play to build skills and confidence.

Contract (psychological or written)

Promote a physical touch between participants. (E.g., hand shake, or hand slap "five") Note that this touch must be positive and genuine, or more mediation may be needed.

Assertiveness Using "I Messages"

Assertiveness is based on the ability to communicate what you want, need and feel without attacking the other person. Assertiveness involves an element of risk. Weighing the risk(s) involved in the situation and/or relationship is an important step in making the decision to disclose information about your feelings, needs and wants.

When the decision is made to act assertively, use words that do not insult or blame the other person. *Note*: When words describe feelings, behaviors and needs, they often <u>feel</u> less threatening or judgmental.

> *Example 1:* " When you copy my paper (describes the behavior), I feel nervous and angry (describes your feelings) because the teacher might see what is happening and I could get a zero (describes the effect the behavior could have)."

Notice the difference in approach when the same issue is addressed in an insulting, judgmental way.

> *Example 2:* "You idiot! You must be stupid or something trying to copy my paper."

Read each situation aloud to the group. Ask a volunteer to restate the message assertively as in example 1.

1. A kid just broke in line in front of you. You've been waiting in line a long time and are fearful they'll run out of tickets.

2. Your best friend shared with another friend something you had told her in confidence.

3. You were punished for being tardy to the class for the first time but John is routinely late and never receives any punishment.

4. You are accused of flirting when you're talking with your friends' boyfriend/girl friend.

5. You are riding in a car on the interstate, and the driver is reckless and exceeding the speed limit.

6. Your parents are out of town and your friends want to have a party at your house.

7. You care deeply for your boyfriend and you do not believe in premarital sex. He is putting pressure on you.

8. You are a good athlete in softball and enjoy it. A coach keeps pressuring you to try out for basketball but you really aren't interested and would rather devote your time to softball and keeping your grades up.

9. Your mother keeps treating you like a baby by reminding you of your homework, chores, etc.

10. One of your close friends is a minority and the group you're with is telling racist jokes.

"Bully Fighting"

(What to do when someone is bothering you)

Don't be too strong

By telling an adult every time the person bothers you.

By pushing or hitting the person.

Don't be too weak

By letting the person keep bothering you without doing something about it.

By showing the person can "hurt your feelings" easily.

Do follow these steps

1. Ignore the person
2. Move away from the person
3. Ask politely for the person to stop
4. Tell the person firmly to quit
5. Give a warning to the person
6. Get help from an adult or other students

Peer Mediation

Mediation is a structured process through which disputants, with the help of mediators:

     a. Identify conflict and its underlying issues;

     b. Examine options and consequences, and

     c. Agree upon a solution.

Benefits of Peer Mediation

1. Allows for more appropriate and effective ways of dealing with suspensions expulsions and detentions in the school setting.

2. Reduces the number of school-based disputes.

3. Improves communications and the climate within the school and community.

4. Decreases level of tension among youth.

5. Binds students to self-generated solutions to problems (ownership).

6. Transfers skills of negotiation to the home.

7. Shifts responsibility for solving appropriate school conflicts from teachers to students and allows teachers to concentrate more on their main task.

Peer Mediation Process

I. **Introducing disputants and peer mediators (adult(s) if present)**
   - Explain process and the role of neutral mediator
   - Get commitment from all parties to work on the issue
   - Discuss confidentiality

II. **Establishing ground rules**
   - One person speaks at a time
   - No name calling
   - No acts of violence
   - Talk to the mediator
   - Applicable school policy

III. **Getting information (facts and feelings)**
   - Allow time to discuss issues and emotions
   - Summarize and clarify
   - Identify each disputant's main concern

IV. **Brainstorming possible solutions**
   - Get ideas for solutions
   - Encourage generation of many options
   - No evaluations at this time
   - Restate and summarize alternatives

V. **Choosing a solution acceptable to both parties**
   - Be specific: who, what, when, why, etc.
   - Check for realistic solutions.
   - Make sure solution is fair and balanced
   - Repeat solutions to disputants
   - Have disputant give feedback on solution

VI. **Contracting for change (the agreement)**
   - Formalize agreement by writing it
   - Have disputant agree to all terms by signing contract
   - Mediators sign contract after disputant

School-wide Strategies for Promoting Conflict Resolution

1. Establish classroom and school-wide norms for behavior and provide many opportunities for intellectual conflicts; (i.e., debates, pro con on issues, elections, etc.)

2. Give opportunities to role play taking different perspectives of the same issue.

3. Develop and teach problem-solving skills.

4. Provide school-wide training on conflict resolution.

5. Create opportunities for researching local, national, international controversies and presenting the diversity of perspectives.

6. Promote cooperative learning in classrooms.

7. Set up a peer mediation program.

8. Teach communication and refusal skills.

9. Promote self responsible behavior (locus of control).

10. Provide positive adult role models.

11. Teach decision-making and goal setting skills.

12. Provide a caring, nurturing environment for staff and students.

13. Interview early in unhealthy conflicts.

14. Provide instruction in the management of anger.

15. Provide additional support and programs for identified at-risk students.

16. Involve parents and community.

17. Collaborate with human service agencies for services and referrals.

18. Develop a student assistance program for early intervention and case management of aggressive, violent students.

Despite your best efforts at preventing the occurrence of a crisis event, it is likely that you will experience some level of crisis in your classroom or school. There are ways to prepare yourself to be able to handle these situations, to enhance the comfort and security of everyone involved. Remember, the Chinese symbol for "crisis" is a combination of the symbols for "danger" and "opportunity." So, in the spirit of looking for both safety and opportunity…

Planning Ahead
It is important to prepare yourself mentally and skill-wise for the possibility of a crisis. When we are stressed we tend to revert to more habitual responses. If we prepare, and rehearse, we are more likely to respond with effective ways of handling any situation.

"When things are steep, remember to stay level-headed."

Horace

Section VI:

Managing & Surviving Classroom Crises

Recognize and Respond to the Precursors to Violence

Following the maxim that **"an ounce of prevention is worth a pound of cure,"** one is always better off learning to recognize the signs that a violent episode is likely, and responding prior to the incident occurring. Anyone who has had to deal with the emotional and physical stress of a violent incident can attest to the fact that it is time consuming and energy draining. The effort that goes into prevention doesn't compare. Following are some of the more common indicators of and precursors to violence.

Anxiety - Distraction

Behaviors that indicate anxiety or distraction may be red flags that emotions are running hot. The individual who is anxious or edgy may be telling you that they are emotionally aroused about something, are feeling vulnerable, and are likely to become more irrational. What are some signs of anxiety?

How do you respond?

Showing concern or support often will defuse an individual who is aroused.

The Direct or Implied Threat

There are times when someone may directly threaten you, or suggest a more indirect threat. "I'm not going to put up with your crap anymore!" "We'll see if you do that again." "You won't have to worry about me anymore after today." The threat usually forecasts harm to yourself or the person doing the threatening. Think of a time you have been threatened.

How should you respond to a threat?

Always respond as though it could happen - by communicating that it is possible, you show respect for the emotions that are driving the individual. If you minimize, or deny the possibility, you may cause the individual to conclude that they need to carry out the threat to show you that they were serious about their motivations.

Ensuring Safety - The First Consideration

Your firmest commitment should be to the safety of all - the innocent students in the area, the student who is the object of aggression, the student who is the aggressor, and to yourself. Property can be replaced; do not sacrifice the safety of any individual to save property.

Physical interventions should be made only for reasons of personal safety. Generally you should not physically intervene to force compliance or to save property (there are exceptions to every rule; young children sometimes need to be restrained to prevent dangerous situations; gently physically moving some young children through an event may be appropriate). Realize that whenever you become physical, you increase the chance that the individual will escalate.

Developing an Effective Classroom Crisis Plan

If a crisis situation begins to develop in your class there are several considerations to be made:

Always Get Help

Your "pre-planning" should include a discussion with individuals who work near you to solicit, and offer, help for dealing with crisis situations. You should have an agreement in place for how to communicate the need for help, what type of help you need, and when you need it. Do not hesitate to call for the help; if it is not needed, no harm is done. If you needed help but didn't get it, harm may occur!

Think of your work setting. Who is available to help if you need someone quickly?

Think of five ways you could communicate with someone to request help.

Isolate

It is often helpful to isolate the individual who is escalating. You have the choice of removing others (including yourself), or removing the one who is escalating. Your intentions are:
- to remove others who may be harmed
- remove the audience
- separate the ones who are in conflict
- create a more private environment for resolving the problem

Use Verbal Interventions First

Calm, deliberate verbal interventions are always preferable to physical interventions. Appropriate verbal skills may include:
- supportive listening
- reflective listening
- restating rules or expectations
- reminding of the consequences
- redirecting the activity
- reframing the activity

Be Aware of Your Physical Messages
- What is your body language saying?
- Are you aware of the need for personal space?
- What is the tone of your voice saying?

Know Yourself

Your effectiveness in implementing a well thought out management plan, or in responding to students who are escalating or behaving violently, will be influenced by your own instincts, style, and preparation. We all tend to regress toward more instinctive responses when we are under pressure - we tend to think less and act more. To maximize your ability to deal with stressful situations, including a crisis or violent episode, it is necessary to:

1. Understand yourself - How do you typically respond to a stressful situation?

2. Study effective ways of responding to stressful situations.

3. Rehearse your newly found strategies and techniques often enough that they begin to become your instinctual response.

4. When an event occurs, review (with yourself or with someone else) how you responded to the situation. What do you feel good about? What would you do differently the next time?

5. Take care of your feelings about the situation.

How we feel, respond to situations, relate to individuals, relate to groups, deal with pressure - all are important to understand to increase our effectiveness in helping youth minimize violence. Following are some questions to prod your thinking about your own responses to a crisis situation. To add a dose of "honesty" to your answers, first make brief notes about three incidents that you have experienced that included aggression, violence, or the potential to become a crisis.

Crisis Incidents I Have Experienced

Incident	How did I respond?
1. _____	_____
_____	_____
_____	_____
2. _____	_____
_____	_____
_____	_____
3. _____	_____
_____	_____
_____	_____
4. _____	_____
_____	_____
_____	_____

Summarize your pattern of responses to the above incidents.

Crisis Response Style Questionnaire

1. Do I tend to want to escape the situation ("flight") or do I prefer to confront the situation head on ("fight")?

2. What role do I typically play in a group? Leader? Follower? One who goes to get help?

3. How do I respond when I am fearful?

4. Do I get angry and feel personally challenged when students become aggressive?

5. What are my "hot buttons"? What really makes me mad?

6. Am I comfortable working with others or do I prefer to handle things alone?

7. What do I believe about why people change?
   - ☞ "people only change if they want to change"
   - ☞ "rules and consequences are the only way to get people to change"
   - ☞ "you have to have a strong person in charge to make others change"
   - ☞ "people will learn from their mistakes if given a chance"
   - ☞ "people are more likely to change if they respect the person who is trying to get them to change"

8. From answering the questions above, what is my greatest asset in handling a crisis situation?

9. How can I enhance or improve my asset(s)?

10. What is my greatest liability in handling a crisis situation?

11. How can I minimize or eliminate my liability(ies)?

In order to be most effective in your responses to a crisis or violent episode, remember to plan ahead, work with others in a team approach, try not to take things personally, and be aware of your assets and liabilities. The importance of practicing or rehearsing your responses is critical!

How to Stay on "Track"

Training, planning, being prepared

Plan ahead by enhancing your skills and understanding through personal study and training.

Rehearsing, practicing, thinking through how you might handle it

Physical rehearsal and mental practice will make it more likely that, when under pressure, you respond with a useful plan.

Ask for help, support form others - rely on your team

The out-of control individual will fell less challenged by a team. And the team members will feel less threatened and more versatile!

Cues - look for signs of anxiety, "red flags"

Responding early is always preferable! Don't wish that the situation will just fade away - respond!

Keep aware of your own instincts and skills - don't overreact

Take time, consciously focus on what you know instead of what you feel.

Handling More Severe Student Aggression and/or Violence

Students come with their own driving forces. Though you may implement your classroom crisis plan perfectly, intervening in textbook fashion to de-escalate the situation, you may experience a more full blown crisis event.

Your role in the evolution of a crisis incident

Understanding how a crisis incident evolves and the role that you play in the event is critical in achieving the greatest safety and security for everyone involved. As an event unfolds, your responses may serve to escalate or calm the person who is acting out. It is important to explore how your responses might impact on the crisis incident.

The Crisis Event

If you closely examine a crisis incident you will discover that the event has a "history". Careful analysis will show that there were events that came first, events in the middle, and events that happened near the end of the incident. For the individual who is acting out, the event includes an evolving set of emotions, as well as behaviors.

To visualize the sequence of events in an incident, examine the following graph.

Graph of a Crisis Event

Physical/Verbal Peak

Escalation ⟶

De-Escalation Phase

Anxiety/Trigger
Events/Provocation

Baseline - Normal

Return to
Baseline - Normal

During this sequence of escalation, what should I do?

As an individual escalates the person responding to the escalation needs to vary their behavior. The goal ALWAYS is to calm things down without a full-blown acting out incident. In spite of the most talented efforts, if the event continues to escalate, the goal is to keep everyone as safe as possible. After the event, the goal is to handle things in such a way that the acting out individual can learn from the experience, thus decreasing the likelihood of a repeat of the incident. Following is an explanation of each phase of a crisis event, including recommended responses or "postures" to be taken (much of this information comes from the National Crisis Prevention Institute's work on crisis prevention).

Baseline - "Normal"

The normal level of behavior for the individual.

Response
- Routine, but with "Feelers"
  Lead the group, using your basic package of ongoing management and leadership skills, but with your "feelers" out to sense anything out of the ordinary with any of your students. Respond early to signs of escalation.

Anxiety/Trigger Events/Provocation

The trigger events or provocations that influence an individual to act out; generally, even if the provocations are not easily observed, physical cues, or signs of anxiety showing that the individual is agitated are readily observable.

Response
- Support
  Give the individual support; let them know that you are sensitive to their needs; a simple, "you look like something is bothering you" may be enough to calm things down.

Escalation

The individual is agitated, beginning to behave irrationally, overreacting to others. Verbally and physically threatening behaviors may be seen.

Responses
- Set limits
- Discretely Remove Items that could be used as weapons
- Get help
- Remove others -get rid of the audience
- Isolate the one who is escalating

Physical/Verbal Peak

The peak of destructive energy; time of most violence. With some, limited to verbal outbursts, with others may become physical.

Responses

- Remove others/isolate the one acting out
- Get help
- Rely on a team approach to physically intervene
- Use physical intervention for physical safety

De-Escalation

The acting out individual begins to calm down. The peak requires a great expenditure of energy; often it only lasts a brief moment before the individual starts settling down.

Response

- Communication
  While it may be tempting to escalate into a punitive outrage at this point, recognize that the individual is still highly vulnerable to re-escalation. Your goal should continue to be the safety of all involved, in the present and future sense. You want to maintain and strengthen bridges of communication. Be calm, don't talk too much, show concern for the safety of all involved. Begin to explore the event - what were the motivations? Were there other ways to address the situation?

In your efforts to maintain communication, don't avoid the fairness of consequences. It is fair and comforting to maintain the consistency of following through on consequences. Make sure that it happens, calmly and respectfully.

Return To Baseline

The individual calms down; though the verbal and/or physical outburst seems to be over, the individual is susceptible to escalating again.

Response

- Follow through on consequences
- Continue a supportive posture
- Show concern for "self-control" with the individual

Prepare yourself for the possibility of physical intervention.

If you think that you may choose, or have to use, physical intervention, remove items from your pockets or person that could injure you or the other individuals (e.g., pencils in the pocket, glasses, tie).

Physical Restraint

If you reach the point where physical restraint seems necessary, keep in mind the following "Do's" and "Don'ts."

Do:

✔ Use physical restraint for physical safety.

✔ Learn techniques in advance that are safe.

✔ Emphasize that you are helping the individual regain control.

✔ Rely on the team approach.

✔ Ask a co-worker to step in and help if you feel like you are losing control.

✔ Make sure that you are not in a situation where you are restraining the opposite sex without assistance or observation, particularly with older students.

✔ Be ready to release the student as they regain control.

✔ Be ready to help the student regain control.

✔ Recognize that the student will need to discuss the situation to regain a sense of respect and to be assured about your reasons for the restraint.

✔ Make sure to attend to any injuries.

✔ Document the event carefully (see below).

✔ Talk out your feelings with someone who can give you support.

Don't:

✘ Restrain if you are angry.

✘ Restrain to force compliance.

✘ Rely on students to assist in restraint of another student.

✘ Restrain if you risk significant injury.

✘ Restrain by yourself if a helper is nearby.

Remember to Document Extreme or Physical Situations Carefully.

If a crisis event occurs it is important to document what happened. Anyone who observed the event should also document so that there are a variety of records to more accurately detail what happened.

What Should Be Included in Documentation?

1. Describe objectively what happened.
2. Where did the event occur?
3. What time did the event occur?
4. Who was involved?
5. What were the precipitating events?
6. Who observed any part of the event?
7. Was anyone hurt?
8. How was the event resolved?
9. Were parents informed?
10. Make sure to notify all significant parties and record who was notified.

Glossary

"Peace and justice are two sides of the same coin."

Dwight D. Eisenhower

Abuse   To hurt or injure by maltreatment.

Aggression   Initiation of forceful, usually hostile, action against another (*Webster, 1984*).

Anger   A feeling of extreme displeasure, hostility, indignation, or exasperation toward someone or something (*American Heritage Dictionary, 1976*).

Avoidance   Ignoring or withdrawing from persons or situations.

Conflict   A strong disagreement or collision of values, needs or intentions among individuals, groups, organizations, communities and nations.

Conflict Mediation   When a neutral and impartial third party actively assists two or more individuals to come to a mutually agreed upon resolution.

Extortion   Obtaining money or property by violence or threat of violence or causing someone to do something against his/her will by force or threat of force (*SERVE, 1993*).

Fighting   Mutual participation in an altercation (physical or verbal).

Malicious Harassment Intentionally intimidating or harassing another person because of that person's race, color, sexual orientation, gender, religion, ancestry or national origin (*SERVE, 1993*).

Problem-Solving   Process for reaching a decision or a solution.

Violence

Physical force employed so as to violate, damage or abuse (*Webster, 1984*).

Violence refers to immediate or chronic situations that result in injury to the psychological, social or physical well-being of individuals or groups. Interpersonal violence... is defined as behavior by persons against persons that threatens, attempts or completes intentional infliction of physical or psychological harm (*American Psychological Association Commission on Violence and Youth, 1993*).

"Let us never negotiate out of fear, but, let us never fear to negotiate."

John F. Kennedy

References & Suggested Materials

Annotated Resources

The following list of organizations, publications, and curricula can be used by districts and schools working to reduce school violence. Some of the information and services are offered at no cost; others require payment. Many of the organizations offer useful publications which are described briefly. Note: the description of organizations and publications in this document does not imply an endorsement by YouthLight, Inc.

The American-Arab Anti-Discrimination Committee
4201 Connecticut Ave., NW Suite 500
Washington, DC 20008
(202) 244-2990
The ADC is a civil rights organization devoted to me elimination of discrimination against Arabs and Arab-Americans. It collects and disseminates statistics on Anti-Arab hate crime and maintains a legal services division.

American Bar Association Special Committee on Dispute Resolution
1800 M. Street, NW
Washington, DC 20036
(202) 331-2258
The ABA committee acts as a clearinghouse in the field of school mediation and publishes the *Directory to School Mediation Projects* which is available to schools.

American Jewish Committee Institute of Human Relations
165 East 56th Street
New York, NY 10022
(212) 751-4000
The AJC was established in 1906 as a human relations organization to protect the safety and security of Jews everywhere. Since then, it has expanded its scope to include activities that safeguard the human rights of all American citizens. Forty chapters exist around the U.S. They have developed conflict resolution programs such as "Ethnic Sharing" for use by schools and other institutions.

Boys and Girls Clubs of America
611 Rockville Pike, Suite 230
Rockville, MD 20852
(301) 251-6676
This national nonprofit youth organization provides support services to 1,240 Boys and Girls Club facilities that help over 1.6 million young people nationwide connect with opportunities for personal growth and achievement. It is the only major nationwide youth agency with a primary mission of service to disadvantaged girls and boys.

Bureau of Alcohol, Tobacco and Firearms
U.S. Treasury Department
650 Massachusetts Ave., NW
Washington, DC 20226
(202) 927-7777
BATF operates a hotline, 800-ATF-GUNS, that individuals can call to report possible firearms and drug or gang activity and other crimes. Agents staffing the hotline share the
tips with local, state, and federal law enforcement agencies.

Bureau of Justice Assistance Clearinghouse
Box 6000
Rockville, MD 20850
(800) 688-4252
This clearinghouse provides information and publications on BJA-funded anti-crime and anti-drug programs, including formula grants, technical assistance, training and demonstration projects. Seven federal clearinghouses can be reached by calling (800) 788-2800. Of special interest to educators are the National Clearinghouse for Alcohol and Drug information, the Drugs and Crime Data Center, the Drug Abuse Information and Referral Hotline, the Drug Information Strategy Clearinghouse, and the National Criminal Justice Reference Service.

Center for Democratic Renewal
PO Box 50469
Atlanta, GA 30302
(404) 221-0025
The Center is a national civil rights organization that monitors white supremacists and far right activities. It also helps communities in combating hate violence.

Center to Prevent Handgun Violence
1225 I Street, NW
Washington, DC 20005
(202) 289-7319

This organization provides educational materials and programs for adults and children on preventing gun deaths and injuries. It offers information about children and gun violence, firearm homicide, suicide, and unintentional shootings, violence in schools, black-on-black violence, and conflict resolution.

Children's Creative Response to Conflict
Box 271
523 North Broadway
Nyack, NY 10960
(914) 358-4601

CCRC offers workshops in creative conflict resolution for children and people who work with children, emphasizing themes of cooperation, communication, affirmation (building self-esteem), and conflict resolution. They also publish a source book of activities, *The Friendly Classroom for a small Planet.*

Intercultural Communication Institute
8835 Southwest Canyon Lane, Suite 238
Portland, OR 97225
(503) 297-4622

The Intercultural Communication Institute is a nonprofit organization designed to foster an awareness and appreciation of cultural differences. The Institute is based on the belief that education and training in intercultural communication will improve competence in dealing with cultural diversity and minimize destructive conflicts among national, cultural, and ethnic groups. It provides technical assistance to schools and groups on a variety of topics related to intergroup relations.

Kids + Guns = A Deadly Equation
1450 Northeast 2nd Avenue
Room 523A
Miami, FL 33132
(305) 995-1986

This program is designed to teach young children the dangers of playing with or carrying weapons. School-based, the program helps K-12 students learn to avoid weapons.

Southern Poverty Law Center
400 Washington Avenue
Montgomery, AL 36104
(205) 264-0286
The Southern Poverty Law Center, founded in 1971, is a nonprofit foundation supported by private donations. The Center's Klanwatch Project was formed in 1980 to help curb Ku Klux Klan and racist violence through litigation, education, and monitoring. Since 1980, lawsuits brought by SPLC and Klanwatch have resulted in federal civil rights indictments against numerous hate groups around the nation.

Male Health Alliance for Life Extension
10 Sunnybrook Road
PO Box 1409
Raleigh, NC 27620
(919) 250-4535
The MHALE Program targets at-risk African-American males aged 11-17 and provides life skills training, vocational education and counseling, conflict-resolution training, and remedial basic education.

National Association for Mediation in Education
425 Amity Street
Amherst, MA 01002
(413) 545-2462
NAME is a national clearinghouse for information about conflict-resolution programs in schools.

National Institute Against Prejudice and Violence
710 Lombard Street
Baltimore, MD 21201
(410) 706-5170
The purpose of the Institute is to study and respond to the problem of violence and intimidation motivated by racial, religious, ethnic, or anti-gay prejudice. Activities include collecting , analyzing, producing, and disseminating information and materials on programs of prevention and response. The Institute conducts research on the causes and prevalence of prejudice and violence and their effects on victims and society; provides technical assistance to public agencies, voluntary organizations, schools, and communities in conflict; analyzes and drafts model legislation; conducts educational and training programs; and sponsor conferences, symposia, and other forums for information exchange among experts.

National Institute for Dispute Resolution
1901 L Street, NW, Suite 600
Washington, DC 20036
(202) 466-4764

This organization works to enhance the understanding acceptance, and development of a spectrum of tools to resolve conflict, including mediation, arbitration, and negotiation. Among its current grant programs and initiatives are Mediation in Schools, Community-Based Dispute Resolution Centers, Court-Based Dispute Resolution Programs, and Statewide Offices of Mediation.

National Victims Resource Center
Box 6000-AJE
Rockville, MD 20850
(800) 627-6872 or
(301) 251-5525/5519

The NVRC is a national clearinghouse for victims' information funded by the Office of Victims of Crime, base that indexes more than 7,000 victim-related books and articles with information on child physical and sexual abuse, victims' services, domestic violence, victim-witness programs, and violent crime.

Project RAP (Reaching Adulthood Prepared)
380 Timothy Road
Athens, GA 30606
(706) 549-1435

Project RAP is a mentoring program for black youth age 12-17 which uses church and community volunteers as role models and mentors.

Violence Intervention Program
Durham Public Schools
PO Box 30002
Durham, NC 27702
(919) 560-2035

Designed to help at-risk elementary school children, the VIP program pairs children with teachers who help them with conflict mediation and resolution skills and also serve as peer counselors and tutors.

Violence Prevention Program
Mecklenburg County Health Department
249 Billinsley Road
Charlotte, NC 28211
(704) 336-5497
This country program teachers conflict resolution skills to seventh through ninth graders and serves as a support group for the youth.

YES! Atlanta
995 Spring Street
Atlanta, GA 30309
(404) 874-6996
This project provides mentoring, tutoring, and job skills training to youth aged 13 to 18 who live in housing projects.

The Youth Gang Drug Prevention Program
Mechlenburg County Health Department
249 Billingsley Road
Charlotte, NC 28211
(704) 336-6443
Designed to help steer youth ages 10-18 away from gang membership, this program sponsors recreation activities and education in conflict resolution for youth and their families.

Publications, Guidebooks, and Curricula

Alternative to Suspension by the Florida Department of Education, 1991. This publication offers many alternatives to out-of-school suspension and expulsion and examines how schools can take steps to reduce overall school violence. Published by the Center for Prevention and Student Assistance, Florida Department of Education, Room 414 Florida Education Center, 325 West Gaines Street, Tallahassee, FL 32399-0400 (904) 488-6315.

Alternative to Violence curriculum by Peace Grows, Inc. Peace Grows publishes several curriculum guides and other publications designed to reduce youth violence through mediation. The organization also offers a number of training packages, ranging from four to forty hours in length. Publications and training examine violence at all levels-from the interpersonal to the international-are aimed at promoting pacifism, and contain useful activities for high school students. Published by Peace Grows, Inc., 513 W. Exchange Street, Akron, OH 44302 (216) 864-5442.

Anger: The Misunderstood Emotion by Carol Tarvis, 1982. A witty and highly readable survey of research that challenges nearly all commonly held assumptions about anger. Published by Simon and Schuster, New York.

Appreciating Differences: Teaching and Learning in a Culturally Diverse Classroom by Eleven Plumes-Device, 1992. This publication, from the SouthEastern Regional Vision for Education *Hot Topics: Usable Research* series, is a practical guidebook for helping teachers infuse their curricula with a multi-cultural perspective. In addition to descriptions of many exemplary school programs and lists of resources and contacts, the publication offers several dozen multi-cultural activities, lessons, games and projects that can be used with students of various ages. Published by SERVE, 345 S. Magnolia Drive, Suite D-23, Tallahassee, FL 32301-2950 (800) 352-6001.

Celebrating Diversity by D. Powers, 1990. This publication is a presentation manual for conducting a day-long training session in appreciating cultural diversity. Produced by the Equal Education Opportunity Program, Florida Department of Education Center, 325 West Gaines Street, Tallahassee, FL 32399-0400.

Challenging Racism by D. Powers, 1990. This publication is a presentation manual for conducting a day-long training session on addressing the problem of racism. Produced by the Equal Education Opportunity Program, Florida Department of Education, Suite 325 West Gaines Street, Tallahassee, FL 32399-0400.

Children of War by Roger Rosenblatt, 1983. The author has traveled widely to discover what children in war-torn countries think and fell about the violence around them. The children he interviews shine through as champions of order in the midst of chaos, quietly resistant to adult attempts to use their tragedies as tools of ideology or instruments of revenge. Published by Anchor Press/Doubleday, New York.

Conflict Resolution Curriculum Packet by Tom and Frances Bigda-Peyton. Designed by high school teachers to teach high school students the basics of conflict resolution, this resource clearly demonstrates how conflict-resolution skills can be applied at all levels. Published by Boston-Area Educators for Social Responsibility, 11 Garden Street, Cambridge, MA 02138.

Creative Conflict Resolution: Over 200 Activities for Keeping Peace in the Classroom by William J. Kreidler. Although designed as a guide to conflict resolution in the elementary classroom, this resource contains many activities that can be easily adapted to the high school level. Published by Goodyear Books, Scott, Foresman and Company, 1990 East Lake Avenue, Glenview, IL 60025.

Cross-Cultural Communication: An Essential Dimension of Effective Education, by Orlando Taylor, 1987. Produced by the Mid-Atlantic Center for Race Equity, American University, 5010 Wisconsin Avenue, NW, #310, Washington, DC 20016.

Developing Personal and Social Responsibility: A Guide for Community Action, by D. R. Grossnickle, and R.D. Stpehens, 1992. Published by the National School Safety Center, Malibu, California.

Discipline Strategies for Teachers (Fastback #344) by Eleanor Barron, 1992. Intended primarily for student teachers and beginning teachers, this document provides practical strategies for both classroom management and discipline. Theory is illustrated in scenarios using positive and negative examples. Published by Phi Delta Kappa Educational Foundation, Bloomington, Indiana.

Effective Strategies for School Security by P.D. Blauvelt, 1981. Published by the National Association of Secondary School Principals, Reston, Virginia (ERIC Document Reproduction Service No. ED 209 774).

Gang Awareness and Intervention: Activities for Elementary and Middle School Students. Published by the Child Development Specialist Program at the Portland Public Schools, Office of Public Information, PO Box 3107, Portland, OR 97222.

Getting to Yes: Negotiating Agreements Without Giving In by Roger Fisher and William Ury, 1981. A fascinating introduction to conflict resolution by two of the field's experts. Published by Houghton Mifflin, Boston.

Guidelines for Policies Addressing Sexual Misconduct Toward Students in Public Schools, 1992. This publication offers clear and direct guidelines for procedures to be adopted to address the concerns surrounding sexual harassment in schools. Overviews of major court cases in the area of sexual harassment in schools are also included as well as a number of newspaper articles on the subject. Published by the Florida Department of Education, PL08, The Capitol, Tallahassee, FL 32399 (904) 487-1785.

Hate Crime: Sourcebook for Schools by C. Bodinger-DeUriate, and A.R. Santo, 1992. A comprehensive examination of the problem of hate crimes in America, this publication details the roots, nature and scope of the problem and offers practical suggestions for reducing hate crimes. Published by Research for Better Schools, 444 North 3rd Street, Philadelphia, PA 19123.

"Human Relations Education: Teaching Non-Violent Solutions to Human Problems" by Ruth Gudinas, *Forum*, Summer 1987. Gudinas discusses how educators can teach about human conflicts and how the process should expand as children become young adults. She also includes information on how to help children learn about alternatives that they can use to resolve conflict peacefully.

I AM Somebody: A Comprehensive Guide to Educate Youth about the Seriousness of Gang Involvement by Clarence Hill, Gang Consultant (middle and high school levels). Published by the Portland Redirection Program, 1032 North Sumner. Portland, OR 97217.

Interagency Collaboration: Improving the Delivery of Services to Children and Families by Stephanie Kadel, 1992. This publication, from the SERVE Hot Topics: Usable Research series, is a practical guidebook for establishing or expanding collaborative efforts to provide services to children and families at a single, easily accessible site such as a school. Many examples are offered of communities and schools that have had success in this effort, and resources and contacts are provided far additional information. Available from SERVE, 345 South Magnolia Drive, Suite D-23, Tallahassee, FL 32301-2950 (800) 352-6001.

Nobody Like a Bully. Published by the School of Education, Winthrop College, Rock Hill, SC 29733 (803) 323-2151.

Peacemaking by Barbara Stanford, 1976. A comprehensive introduction to conflict resolution by a leading educator in the field. Contains many exercises that can be used with high school students. Published by Bantam Books, New York.

Peer Leader Training Manual - Three Session Curriculum for Teaching Adolescents by C. Sousa, L. Bancroft, & T. German, 1991. Published by the Dating Violence Instruction Project, c/o Transition House, P.O. Box 530, Harvard Square Station, Cambridge, MA 02238.

Preventing Family Violence by the Family Violence Curriculum Project. A comprehensive, useful, and sensitively designed curriculum dealing with such controversial issues as family violence, child sexual abuse, and date rape. Published by Massachusetts Department of Public Health, Resource Center for the Prevention of Family Violence, 150 Tremont Street, Boston, MA 02111.

Preventing Teen Dating Violence - Three Session Curriculum for Teaching Adolescents by C. Sousa, L. Bancroft, & T. German, 1991. Published by the Dating Violence Instruction Project, c/o Transition House, P.O. Box 530, Harvard Square Station, Cambridge, MA 02238.

The Prevention of Youth Violence: A Framework for Community Action by the Center for Environmental Health and Injury Control, Division of Injury Control at the Centers for Disease Control, 1992. This manual is designed to help reduce violence and prevent injuries and deaths from violence among youths in their community. It is based on principals of effective, community-based health promotion programs that address a variety of chronic diseases as well as problems of youth such as sexually transmitted diseases and teenage pregnancy. Published by Centers for Disease Control, Atlanta, Georgia.

Safe and Alive by Terry Dobson with Judith Shepard-Chow, 1981. This guide to protecting self and property contains a very clear and practical discussion of fight, flight, and other options. Dobson is a martial arts expert. Published by J.P. Tarcher, Los Angeles.

Safe Passage on City Streets by Dorothy T. Samuel, 1975. An optimistic and easy-to-read book of experiences in which people have countered violence with non-violence — good for use with students. Published by Abingdon Press, Nashville, Tennessee.

School Safety and Security Management. Published by Rusting Publications, 403 Main Street, Port Washington, NY 11050 (516) 883-1440.

School Safety World. Published by National Safety Council, 444 North Michigan Avenue, Chicago, IL 60601.

School Safety Check Book, 1990. Published by National School Safety Center, Malibu, California.

School Safety Journal and National School Safety Center Report. This periodical offers timely information on school violence prevention efforts around the nation. Published by the National School Safety Center, 4165 Thousand Oaks Boulevard, Suite 290, Westlake Village, CA 91362 (818) 377-6200.

Second Step: A Violence Prevention Curriculum. This curriculum is designed fro grades 1-3, 4-5, and 6-8. Published by Committee for Children, 172, 20th Avenue, Seattle, WA 98122 (206) 322-5050.

Set Straight on Bullies by S. Greenbaum, B. Turner, and R.D. Stephens, 1989. This resource contains valuable information about what causes children to become bullies, the harm they can cause to other children, and ways to reduce this damaging phenomenon. Published by National School Safety Center, Malibu, California.

Special Focus. Preventing Violence: Program Ideas and Examples, 1992. This booklet presents a cross-section of anti-violence programs representing a broad spectrum of partners, audiences, and long-and short-term efforts to address violence concerns in communities. Published by the National Crime Prevention Council, Washington, D.C.

Violence and Aggression by Ronald H. Bailey, 1976. An excellent and readable summary of research in the area. Its use of illustrations make it a good resource for students as well. Published by Time-Life Books, New York.

Violence Prevention: Curriculum for Adolescents by Deborah Prothrow-Stith, 1987. This curriculum guide contains sample lessons, exercises, projects, and handouts to help teachers and students address the issues of violence. Its goal is to help students to become more aware of positive ways to deal with anger and arguments, how fights begin and escalate, and non-violent choices for conflict situations. A set of sixteen handouts is included. Published by Education Development Center, Incorporated, 55 Chapel Street, Newton, MA 02160.

Who's Hurt and Who's Liable? Sexual Harassment in Massachusetts Schools. A Curriculum and Guide for School Personnel, by F. Klein and N. Wilber, 1986. A curriculum and guide for all members of the school community, this publication defines sexual harassment, explains the legal issues involved, describes administrative strategies, and presents students activities and classroom lessons on the subject. Published by the Massachusetts Department of Education, 1385 Hancock Street, Quincy, MA 02169.

Additional Resources

American Bar Association Standing Committee on Dispute Resolution
2nd Floor South
1800 M. Street NW
Washington, DC 20036
(202) 331-2258

American Association of Retired Persons Criminal Justice Services
601 E. Street, NW
Building B. Fifth Floor
Washington, DC 20049
(202) 728-4363

American Association of School Administrators
1801 North Moore Street
Arlington, VA 22209
(703) 528-0700

Center for Research on Aggression
Syracuse University
805 South Crouse Avenue
Syracuse, NY 13244-2280
(315) 443-9641

Office of School Safety
New York City Board of Education
600 E. 6th Street
New York, NY 10009
(212) 979-3300

Community Guidance Clinic
Trent and Elva Streets
Durham, NC 27705
(919) 684-3044

Community Relations Service
U.S. Department of Justice
5550 Friendship Boulevard
Suite 330
Chevy Chase, MD 20815
(301) 492-5929

Education Development Center, Inc.
55 Chapel Street
Newton, MA 02160
(617) 969-7100

I Am Somebody, Period, Inc.
851 Pinewell Drive
Cincinnati, OH 45255
(513) 474-4449

Judge Baker Guidance Center
295 Longwood Avenue
Boston, MA 0215
(617) 232-8390

National Alliance for Safe Schools
4903 Edgemoor Lane
Suite 403
Bethesda, MD 20814
(301) 654-2774

National Assault Prevention Center
Post Office Box 02005
Columbus, OH 43202
(614) 291-2540

National Crime Prevention Council
1700 K Street
Washington, DC 20006
(202) 466-6272

National Crime Prevention Institute
Brigman Hall
University of Louisville
Louisville, KY 40292
(502) 588-6987

National Committee for the Prevention of Child Abuse
332 South Michigan Avenue
Suite 1600
Chicago, IL 60604-3817
(312) 633-3520

National Exchange Clubs Foundation for the Prevention of Child Abuse
3050 Central Avenue
Toledo, OH 43606
(419) 535-3232

National McGruff House Network
1879 South Main
Suite 180
Salt Lake City, UT 84115
(801) 486-8768

National Organization for Victim Assistance
1757 Park Road, NW
Washington, DC 20010
(202) 232-6682

National Peer Helpers Association (NPHA)
P.O. Box 2684
Greenville, NC 27834
(919) 522-3959

The National PTA
700 North Rush Street
Chicago, IL 60611-2571
(312) 787-0977

National School Boards Association
1680 Duke Street
Alexandria, VA 22314
(703) 838-67760

National School Safety Center
4165 Thousand Oaks Blvd.
Suite 290
Westlake Village, CA 91362
(805) 373-9977

National Urban League, Inc.
Stop the Violence Clearinghouse
500 East 62nd Street
New York, NY 10021
(212) 310-9000

National Victim Center
309 West 7th Street
Suite 705
Fort Worth, TX 76102
(817) 877-3355

National Helper (Peer Counseling)
Roberts, Fitzmahan and Associates
9131 California Ave., SW
Seattle, WA 98136-2599
(206) 932-8409

Prevention Intervention Program in Trauma, Violence and Sudden Bereavement in Childhood
Dr. Robert S. Pynoos, Director, UCLA
Department of Psychiatry and
Biobehavioral Sciences
750 Westwood Plaza
Los Angeles, CA 90024
(310) 206-8973

Prince George County Public Schools
Peter Blauvelt, Director of Security
507 Largo Road
Upper Marlboro, MD 20722
(301) 336-5400

Society for the Prevention of Violence
3109 Mayfield Road
Room 207
Cleveland Heights, OH 44118
(216) 371-5545

(Sources: Bastian & Taylor, 1991; Bodinger-DeUriarte and Santo, 1992; McMahon et al., 1998; NSSC, 1989, 1990a; Prothrow-Stith, 1987; Roderick, 1987; *Stop the Violence-Start Something, 1991)*

Resources

National Network of Violence Prevention Practitioners

Building Conflict-Solving Skills
Kansas Child Abuse Prevention Council
715 S.W. 10th Street
Topeka, KS 66612
(913) 354-7738
Executive Director: James McHenry
Director/Coordinator: Helen Swan

Community Youth Gang Services,
Project Community Youth Gang
Services, Inc.
144 South Fetterly Avenue
Los Angeles, CA 90022
(213) 266-4264
Executive Director: Steve Valdivia

Conflict Management/Mediation
Program University of Missouri System
1321 South 11th Street
St. Louis, MO 63104

Missouri Department of Health
6090 E. Monroe Street
Jefferson City, MO 65102
(314) 421-6063
(314) 751-6365
Executive Director: Kathleen E. Cain
(Dept. of Health, Office Of Injury Control)
Director/Coordinator: Steve Jenkins
(Univ. of Missouri)

Conflict Resolution Resources for
Schools and Youth The Community
Board Program
1540 Market Street, Room 490
San Francisco, CA 94102
(415) 552-1250
Executive Director: Terry Amsler
Director/Coordinator: Terry Amsler and
Jim Halligan

ESR National Conflict Resolution
Program Educators for Social
Responsibility
23 Garden Street
Cambridge, MA 02138
(617) 492-1764
Executive Director: Ruth Bowman
Director/Coordinator: William J. Kreidler
and Larry Dieringer

Facing History and Ourselves
16 Hurd Road
Brookline, MA 02146
(617) 232-1595
Executive Director: Margot Stern Strom
Director/Coordinator: Marc Skvirsky

Gang Intervention Program
Youth Development, Inc. (YDI)
1710 Centro Familiar, S.W.
Albuquerque, NM 87105
(505) 873-1604
Executive Director: Chris Baca
Director/Coordinator: Ruben Chavez

**Outreach and Tracking Program
Old Colony YMCA**
320 Main Street
Brockton, MA 02401
(508) 584-1100
Executive Director: Larry Cohen
Director/Coordinator: Nancy Baer
and Andres Soto

**Positive Adolescent Choices Training
(PACT) Program
Wright State University**
School of Professional Psychology
110 Health Sciences Building
Dayton, OH 45435
(513) 873-3492
Executive Director: W. Rodney
Hammond
Director/Coordinator: Michelle Hassell

**Resolving Conflict Creatively Program
(RCCP)**
163 Third Avenue, #239
New York, NY 10003
(212) 260-6290
Executive Director: Tom Roderick
Director/Coordinator: Linda Lantieri

**Saturday Institute for Manhood,
Brotherhood, Actualization (SIMBA)
Wholistic Stress Control Institute, Inc.**
3480 Greenbriar Parkway, Suite 310 B
Atlanta, GA 30331
(404) 344-2021
Executive Director: Jennie C. Trotter
Director/Coordinator: Tony R. Graves

**Second Step: A Violence Prevention
Curriculum Committee for Children
(CFC)**
172 20th Ave.
Seattle, WA 98122
(206) 322-5050
Executive Director: Karen Bachelder
Director/Coordinator: Kathy Beland

**Straight Talk About Risks (STAR)
Center to Prevent Handgun Violence**
1225 Eye Street, NW
Suite 1150
Washington, DC 20005
(202) 289-7319
Executive Director: Nancy Gannon
Director/Coordinator: Carolyn Abdullah
and Nancy Gannon

**Targeted Outreach: Gang
Prevention/Intervention Boys and Girls
Clubs of America**
771 First Avenue
New York, NY 10017
(212) 351-5906
Executive Director: Roxanne Spillett

**Teen Dating Violence Program Austin
Center for Battered Women**
Post Office Box 19454
Austin, TX 78760
(512) 928-9070
Executive Director: Mary Robertson
Director/Coordinator: Barri Rosenbluth

**Teen Program Battered Women's
Alternatives**
Post Office Box 6406
Concord, CA 94524
(510) 676-7748
Executive Director: Rollie Mullen
Director/Coordinator: Allan Creighton

Teen's on Target Youth ALIVE
c/o The Trauma Foundation
SF General Hospital Bldg. 1, Rm. 306
San Francisco, CA 94110
(415) 821-8209

**Victim's Service Program: Stop Black-
on-Black Murder Community Mental
Health Council, Inc.**
8704 South Constance Avenue
Chicago, IL 60617
(312) 734-4033 Ext. 156
Executive Director: Carl c. Bell
Director/Coordinator: Denyse Snyder

**Violence Prevention Project
Department of Health and Hospitals**
1010 Mass. Avenue, 2nd Floor
Boston, MA 02118
(617) 534-5196
Executive Director: Linda B. Hudson

**Washington Community Violence
Prevention Program Washington
Hospital Center**
110 Irving Street, NW, Room 4B-46
Washington, DC 20010
(202) 877-3761
Executive Director: Patricia S. Gainer

(Sources: *Connections Newletter of the National Network of Violence Prevention Practitioners.* Newton, MA: Education Development Center, Inc. Vol. 1, Fall 1992.)

Additional Organizations

Alternatives to Violence PEACE GROWS, Inc.
513 West Exchange Street
Akron, OH 44302
(216) 864-5442

Canadian Institute for Conflict Resolution (CIRC)
c/o Saint Paul University
223 Main Street
Ottawa, Ontario, Canada K1S 1C4
(613) 235-5800 (613) 782-3005 (fax)

Holds workshops on peer mediation and conflict resolution. Publishes a newsletter and will refer young people and educators to resource materials.

Child Abuse Program Children's Hospital
700 Children's Drive
Columbus, OH 43205
(614) 461-6888

Clearinghouse on Family Violence
P.O. Box 1182
Washington, DC 20013
(703) 385-7565

National clearinghouse and information center for family violence issues.

Community Mediation Services of Central Ohio
800 Jefferson Avenue
Columbus, OH 43215
(614) 228-7191 (614) 228-7213 (fax)

Community Mediation Services of Central Ohio
800 Jefferson Avenue
Columbus, OH 43215
(614) 228-7191 (614) 228-7213 (fax)

Family Violence Program
c/o Canadian Council on Social Development
55 Parkdale Avenue
P.O. Box 3505 Station C
Ottawa, Ontario, Canada K1Y 4G1
(613) 728-1865

Iowa Peace Institute
P.O. Box 480
Grinnell, IA 50112
(515) 236-4880

Promotes alternative to violent resolution of conflicts. Offers information (books, videos) on all aspects of conflict resolution, in addition to training workshops for teachers.

Kids Against Crime
P.O. Box 22004
San Bernadino, CA 92406
(714) 882-1344

Aids young people in preventing crime.

Manitoba Women's Directorate
Minister Responsible for the Status of Women Legislature Building
Winnipeg, Manitoba, Canada R3C 0V8
(204) 945-3476 (800) 282-8069)

Offers a directory of curricula, information, videos, and books on conflict resolution and violence prevention.

Metropolitan Life Insurance Co., Inc.
New York, NY 10010
(212) 578-2211

"Victory Over Violence" listing for a list
of exemplary programs

National Crime Prevention Council
1700 K Street, NW., Second Floor
Washington, DC 20006
(202) 466-NCPC

National organization provides information, sponsors programs on crime and drug
prevention and other topics.

National School Safety Center
4165 Thousand Oaks Blvd., Suite 290
Westlake Village, CA 91362
(805) 373-9977

National association of school safety personnel. Publishes the *Schools Safety
Update* six times a year. Collects statistics
on school violence and offers printed
resources to educators.

Bibliography for Teachers

Barron, E. (1992). *Discipline Strategies for Teachers. Fast back #344.* Bloomington, IN: Phi Delta Kappa Educational Foundation.

Garbarino, J., Dubrow, N., Kostelny, K., and Pardo, C. *Children in Danger: Coping with Consequences of Community Violence*, San Francisco: Jossey-Bass, 1992.

Hamburg, David A. Today's Children: Creating a Future for a Generation in Crisis. New York and Toronto: Times Books, 1992.

Hechinger, Fred M. *Fateful Choices: Healthy Youth for the 21st Century,* New York: Carnegie Corporation, 1992.

Kreidler, W.J. (1991). *Creative Conflict Resolution: Over 200 Activities for Keeping Peace in the Classroom.* Glenview, IL: Goodyear Books, Scott, Foresman and Company.

Prothrow-Stith, D. (1987). *Violence Prevention: Curriculum for Adolescents.* Newton, MA: Education Development Center.

Prothrow-Stith, D., and Weissman, M. *Deadly Consequences: How Violence is Destroying our Teenage Population and a Place to Begin Solving the Problem.* New York: HarperCollins, 1991.

Rosenberg, M.L., and Fenley, M.A., eds. *Violence in America: A Public Health Approach.* New York: Oxford University Press, 1991.

Bibliography for Students

Biographies and Other Nonfiction

Barry, Kathleen. *Susan B. Anthony: A Biography of a Singular Feminist.* **New York: New York University Press, 1988.**
Details the rise of the Quaker woman who led the suffrage movement and pioneered the rights of women in America.

Bentley, James. *Albert Schweitzer.* **Milwaukee: Gareth Steven, 1988.**
Examines the life of the famous peacemaker and humanitarian, who gave up a life of wealth to spend fifty years tending the sick of Africa and was rewarded with the Nobel Peace Prize.

Cater, Jimmy. *Talking Peace: A Vision for the Next Generation.* **New York: Dutton, 1993.**
Former U.S. president Jimmy Carter examines the causes and effects of conflict and urges nonviolent conflict resolution in today's world. He also recounts his efforts in bringing about peace in various parts of the world.

Denenberg, Barry. *Nelson Mandela: No Easy Walk to Freedom.* **New York: Scholastic, 1991.**
As leader of the African National Congress, Mandela attempted, through peaceful means, to abolish apartheid in South Africa. For his efforts he was imprisoned by the government and released in 1990 after serving 26 years.

Durrell, Ann, and Sachs, Marilyn, eds. *The Big Book for Peace.* **New York, Dutton, 1990.**
Seventeen stories and poems focus on the wisdom of peace and the absurdity of fighting. Selections for grades 3-8. Authors include Natalie Babbitt, Jean Fritz, Katherine Paterson, Yoshiko Uchida, Charlotte Zolotow, and 11 others. Illustrated by Maurice Sendak, Jerry Pinkey, and 16 others.

Ferrell, Frank and Janet. *Trevor's Place.* **San Francisco: Harper & Row, 1985.**
One winter evening in 1983, eleven-year-old Trevor Ferrell saw a story on the news about the homeless. This book documents how his response led to the Trevor Campaign, dedicated to helping the homeless.

Friese, Kai. *Rosa Parks: The Movement Organizes.* **Englewood Cliffs, NJ: Sliver Burdett, 1990.**
A biography of the American-American woman from Alabama whose refusal to give up her seat on a bus is often credited with civil rights movement.

Gray, Charlotte. *Bob Geldof.* **Milwaukee: Gareth Stevens, 1988.**
Part of the People who Have Helped the World series, this title followers the efforts of the musician who organized both the Band Aid and Live Aid projects to benefit the starving people of Africa.

Gray, Charlotte. *Mother Teresa.* **Milwaukee: Gareth Stevens, 1988.**
Chronicles the life of the nun who dedicated her life to the poorest of the poor in the slums of Calcutta, India.

Lucas, Eileen. *Peace on the Playground: Nonviolent Ways of Problem Solving.* **New York: Franklin Watts, 1991.**
The excellent text and photos in this book help middle/junior high school students learn that conflict is normal and can be handled without violence. After outlining a problem-solving approach very similar to that used in *Skills for Adolescence,* the author goes beyond peace on the playground (and in the classroom) to describe ways young people can help bring peace t ome planet.

Martin, Patricia Stone. *Samantha Smith: Young Ambassador.* **Vero Beach, FL: Rourke Enterprises, 1987.**
Part of the Reaching Your Goal series, this simply written biography chronicles the short life of the eleven-year-old girl who wrote Soviet Leader Yuri Andropocv asking for peace. Advice on setting and reaching your own goals is included.

Nicholson, Michael. *Mahatna Gandhi.* **Milwaukee: Gareth Stevens, 1988.**
Follows the life of the statesman who led India in its fight for independence from British rule, creating a revolution without guns and bringing about change through nonviolent means.

Nicholson, Michael, and Winner, David. *Raoul Wallenberg.* **Milwaukee, Gareth Stevens, 1989.**
The story of the Swedish diplomat who used his quick wits to save thousands of Jews from the Nazis during World War II.

Parks, Rosa, and Haskins, Jim. *Rosa Parks: My Story.* **New York: Dial, 1990.**
An icon of the civil rights movement tells what it was like to defy the system and, in the process, become a symbol of freedom for African Americans.

Reef, Catherine. *Henry David Thoreau: A Neighbor to Nature.* **Frederick, MD: Henry Holt and Co., 1992.**
Details the life of the famous pacifist and nature writer who wrote Walden while communing with nature in the New England woods.

Ring, Elizabeth. *Henry David Thoreau: In Step with Nature.* Brookfield, CT: Millbrook Press, 1993.
An introduction, with photos and documents, to the life of the New England philosopher and writer who lived according to a "different drummer."

Rosen, Deborah N. *Anwar el-Sadat: A Man of Peace.* Chicago: Children's Press, 1986.
A biography of the Egyptian president whose efforts to end the Arab-Israeli conflict won him the 1978 Nobel Peace Prize.

Rowland, Della. *Martin Luther King, Jr.: The Dream of Peaceful Revolution.* Englewood Cliffs, NJ: Silver Burdett, 1990.
Recounts the struggle and various influences of the Nobel Peace Prize winner who espoused nonviolence in the civil rights movement. Introduction by Andrew Young.

Schloredt, Valerie. *Martin Luther King, Jr.* Milwaukee: Gareth Steven, 1988.
Summarizes through color photographs and timelines the life of the famous civil rights leader.

Scholes, Katherine, *Peace Begins With You.* San Francisco: Sierra Club Books, 1990.
Thoughtful text and realistic drawing explain that peace means being allowed to be different, conflict can be the beginning of something new and good, and working nonviolently for peace may be harder than using force. For grades 4-8.

Webb, Margot. *Coping with Street Gangs.* New York: Rosen Publishing, 1990.
A realistic guide geared to middle/junior high and high school students. The author discusses why gangs exist, how to resist joining a gang, ways to respond when threatened by one, and ways to get help.

Winner, David. *Desmond Tutu.* Milwaukee: Gareth Stevens, 1989.
while serving as Archbishop of Cape Town, this civil rights leader has worked for a peaceful resolution to the racial strife in South Africa.

Fiction

Cornier, Robert. *Other Bells for Us to Ring.* New York: Delacorte Press, 1990.
Living in Massachusetts during World War II, Darcy learns the differences that divide French-Canadians from Americans, and Protestants from Catholics, along with the fact that war unites all fractions.

Myers, Walter Dean. *Scorpions.* **New York: Harper & Row, 1988.**
As the reluctant leader of a Harlem gang, twelve-year-old Jamal's life is dramatically changed when he acquires a gun. He and his best friend Tito manage to escape the gang, but not before tragic consequences occur.

Spinelli, Jerry. *Maniac Magee.* **Boston: Little Brown, 1990.**
An orphan becomes legendary for various feats, including resolving racial conflict among the young people in a small town. This book, which won the 1991 Newbery Award, has already become a favorite among adolescents.

Videotapes

Available from Quest International

Between You and Me: Learning to Communicate*
Length: 30 minutes   Date: 1990
This video, similar to the "Conflict Resolution" video from Sunburst, is geared to middle/junior high students. Part 1 stresses the importance of clear, concise, and complete communication. Realistic situations also show how conflicting body language and mixed messages confuse listeners - can lead to or escalate conflict. Part 2 demonstrates the active listening techniques covered in Unit 2 of Lions-Quest Skill for Adolescence and "Working Toward Peace." Part 3 explores communication roadblocks and a method of expressing strong feelings similar to the "What, Why, and How" message.

Friendship: The Good Times...The Bad Times*
Length: 24 minutes   Date: 1990
In Part 1, Lisa's mother and brother help her deal with the situation when her best friend likes someone else. Three open-ended vignettes in Part 2 focus on common conflicts in friendship: How loyal should a friend be? How much responsibility does one friend have for another's well-being? Discussion questions will help your students find ways to solve these and related conflicts.

Trouble at School*
Length: 20 minutes   Date: 1991
In interrelated situations, three middle schoolers learn to handle strong emotions, deal with peer rejection, and resist negative peer pressure. A teacher, school counselor, and coach provide thoughtful guidance that also applies to resolving conflicts.

*When There's Trouble at Home**
Length: 35 minutes   Date: 1992
In the first segment, Dad has lost his job and the family is experiencing bitter conflict. A family meeting finally allows both parents and children to express their strong feelings and pull together. In Part 2, Christina's parents have divorced. she has to baby-sit her younger brother in the evenings while Mom works. When her health and grades begin to suffer, a school counselor serves as a mediator in the conflict. In Part 3, two new step-brothers are in conflict over a shared bedroom. Their resentment escalates until their parents help them settle the conflict through compromise.

Available from other sources

Bullets Have No Names on Them
Length: 22 minutes   Date: 1993
Source: Coronet/MTI (800/621-2131)
Real kids describe being shot - or watching the shooting death of someone they loved. Several speak from wheelchairs, paralyzed by stray bullets. This chilling, effective video offers compelling reasons to "put the guns down." It includes interviews with members of the Bloods and Crips from LA, supposedly working together now to stop what even they describe as senseless gun-related violence.

*The Color of Friendship**
Length: 30 minutes   Date: 1981
Source: Coronet/MTI (800/621-2131)
Two boys have a shaky beginning to their friendship after their school is integrated. A series of incidents finally convinces each boy that the other on is not the stereotype he expected. An ABC Afterschool Special.

Conflict Resolution (for students)
Length: 26 minutes   Date: 1992
Source: Sunburst Communications (800/431-1934)
This video is incorporated into several session of "Working Toward Peace" because it reinforces unit concepts. Skits in Part 1 compare three styles of dealing with conflict: avoidance, confrontation, and problem solving. Part 2 stresses the importance of - and techniques for - active listening. Young people are shown how to express their feelings without blaming or accusing by using and "I" message, similar to me "What, Why, and How" message in Skills for Adolescence. Actors in Part 3 demonstrate how mediation works in several situations.

Conflict Resolution (for teachers of grades 5-12)
Length: 24 minutes   Date: 1992
Source: Sunburst Communications (800/431-1934)
this staff development package includes a video, handouts, and suggested activities. It could be used as an orientation to "Working Toward Peace." In the video, teachers in California middle and high schools explain and demonstrate their conflict resolution programs, which include trained peer mediators. Students use active listening and other techniques similar to those taught in "Working Toward peace."

*The Hand-Me-Down Kid**
Length: 31 minutes   Date: 1983
Source: Coronet/MTI (800/621-2131)
Two friends convince 12-year-old Ari to borrow her older sister's bike without permission. The bike is stolen, and Ari makes up a story to hid her involvement. The video explores how peer pressure leads to conflict for both Ari and her friends. An ABC Afterschool Special.

Settling Disagreements, Disputes, and Fights
Length: 40 minutes (5 parts)   Date: 1992
Source: Learning Tree Publishing (303/740-9777)
Part 1 of this excellent video offers many reasons why it's important to learn how to resolve disagreements peacefully so that relationships aren't threatened. The next three parts provide specific, useful, and practical suggestions for keeping disagreements from escalating into fights or feuds, for resolved (such as those that stem from strong beliefs, personality conflicts, or a difference of opinion with an authority figure). Each section ends with discussion questions. Part 5 offers five open-ended conflict scenarios relevant to grades 4-8. Viewers are invited to stop the tape, discuss the situation, and think of ways to resolve it.

*Teens in Changing Families: Making It Work**
Length: 26 minutes   Date: 1989
Source: Sunburst Communications (800/431-1934)
Accepting a new parent and/or new siblings can be difficult. Real people (not actors) in two step/blended families discuss the challenges and conflicts they face and the strategies that help them maintain a rewarding family life.

Understanding Stress
Length: 43 minutes (4 parts)   Date: 1990
Source: Learning Tree Publishing (303/740-9777)
This strong video explores the definition of stress (a physical and mental response to things we believe might do us harm), the effects of short- and long-term stress, and ways to cope with stress (engaging in physical activity, getting involved in hobbies, and/or talking with a parent, friend, teacher, or professional counselor). The narrator emphasizes that stress is a fact of modern life, but we can learn how to deal with it and even use it to our advantage.

Working It Out: Conflict Resolution
Length: 28 minutes   Date: 1992
Source: Sunburst Communications (800/431-1934)
In Part 1 of this video designed for middle schoolers, young people listen to Dr. Advice's radio talk show to hear his excellent guidelines for solving their conflicts. With rap music in the background, Dr. Advice stresses listening to one another and choosing solutions acceptable to everyone involved. The video also shows what happens when young listeners follow his advice. In Part 2, students in conflict over a shared locker end up in detention, where mediation helps them solve their differences.

You Can Refuse
Length: 20 minutes   Date: 1993
Source: The Altschul Group Corporation (800/323-9084)
This strong overview of refusal skills can help students deal with conflicts resulting from negative peer pressure. It includes ways to use refusal skills in difficult situations. The suggested approach includes the following steps:
1. Ask questions.
2. Name the trouble. ("That's dangerous.")
3. State the consequences. ("That will make you sick.")
4. Suggest alternatives.
5. Move it (leave), sell it (convince the other person to join you in a safe activity), leave the door open ("If you change your mind...").

If students are pressured, the video urges them to stay calm; say the person's name and make eye contact; say "listen to me"; pause to see if the person is listening; if not, continue to refuse. If none of this works, young people are encouraged to leave.